KEYS TO THE KINGDOM

FIRST OF A TRILOGY

KEYS TO THE KINGDOM

FIRST OF A TRILOGY

TY MARSHALL

For information contact :

www.tymarshallbooks.com

Cover design by Javier Mercado

ISBN: 978-0-9984419-2-4

First Edition: May 2015

10 9 8 7 6 5 4 3 2 1

PROLOGUE

The familiar scenery brought a wave of nostalgia over Michael Di Toro as he peered through the tinted glass, taking in the sights and sounds of the old neighborhood. He hadn't been back to Howard Beach in what felt like forever and felt the need to do some sightseeing. That included cruising passed the social club on the corner of Coleman Square and 159th Avenue that once served as his headquarters for all his illegal activities. Not much had changed about the predominately Italian neighborhood since he had relocated following Hurricane Sandy, with the exception of a few locally owned businesses being replaced by chain stores. But the trip down memory lane was exactly what he needed at the moment; it brought a much needed smile across his face.

Iron Mike, as he was referred to in the streets because of the way he ruled with an iron fist, had overseen one of the bloodiest takeovers in New York City's recent history and he loved every minute of it. He also enjoyed the spotlight that came with being a celebrity gangster and would often scan the newspaper looking for his name. Di Toro had instructed all of his soldiers to carry out hits in public, creating an atmosphere of constant fear as he seized control. In a place renowned for its legendary criminals he ranked near the top as the reputed boss of the most ruthless regime in the city, the Martello family. For years they had moved large amounts of cocaine from Miami up the east coast into New York, murdering rivals and stacking millions in the process. The arrogant Mafioso led a group of blood thirsty enforcers who didn't believe in leniency nor second chances. When debtors refused or couldn't pay up they quickly, felt his wrath. He had a thing for torture, loving to see them suffer before he eventually put them out of their misery.

Di Toro's reign had made him a very rich and powerful man but had nearly destroyed the unification of "The Five Families" of New York, weakening the others through murder and his refusal to spread the wealth in pursuit of becoming "capo di tutti capi", Boss of all Bosses. Iron Mike had definitely left his mark on the Big Apple, making him a wanted man by the feds and enemies alike.

That was why the precautionary measures taken for this trip were vital. He had flown on a private jet into a nondescript private airport out in Long Island and was riding in a bullet proof SUV with the tightest of security in tow. But it was a risk he was willing to take, this wasn't a triumphed return of the king coming home to reclaim his throne, it was a sad one.

He had returned to lay his mother to rest. There wasn't a federal agent or rival gangster on earth that could keep him away. The love he had for her took precedence over any concern he may have had for his own life.

The funeral was just about to begin as the SUV he was riding in pulled into St. John Cemetery in Queens. Mike patiently watched from a distance as the mourners there to pay their respects gradually filled up the empty seats. As his vehicle slowly came to a stop, only feet from what was to be his mother's final resting place, Mike finally got a glimpse of the casket. The custom bronze finished casket with rich, dark russet shades sat surrounded by an assortment of floral arrangements that had been sent by those who had loved and cherished her throughout her lifetime. Many saw the funeral as an opportunity to get noticed by the head of the family, sending large expensive arrangements hoping to land in his good graces. The smell of the flowers mixed with the bright sun on an unusually warm fall afternoon gave the scene a heartwarming feel. Mike fought back tears as the harsh reality began to set in. He was there to say goodbye to the one person in the world that loved him unconditionally. From his earliest run-ins with the law, she had never wavered with her love and support for him. He may have been a psychopath to the rest of the world but to her he was still just Little Mikey. A cold-blooded killer whose heart was black as night; he held a special place in it for her that hadn't been consumed by his wicked ways. He knew he was responsible for the looks of disgust she received from her neighbors and church members. The things they read in the newspapers about him were sickening but he always admired how she never showed an ounce of disappointment in any of his actions.

The doors of the SUV swung open and three armed men dressed in dark colored suits spilled out and were joined by another group of men, also armed, that had exited the two SUVs that had accompanied him. Finally, one of the men opened the door allowing Mike to step out of the truck and all eyes were immediately focused on him. Dressed in a tailored black suit, black dress shirt and tie, all courtesy of Giorgio Armani, the stylish 53-year old looked more like a CEO of Fortune 500 company than the commander in chief of a criminal enterprise.

Mike walked down the aisle as every eye remained glued to him, slowly approaching the casket with a few of his soldiers shadowing his every move. He turned to the stocky built man on his right and whispered something in his ear while pointing to a group of people seated in the front row of mourners. The man immediately turned and gestured to another one of Mike's men to clear those seats, as that was where the boss intended to sit. Mike continued his trek to the casket with his men closely shadowing him.

"Can I get some privacy here?" he sarcastically asked in his thick Italian accent, as he noticed how close his soldiers were to him. Hoping to say his last regards without the men hovering over him. The two men in front nodded and receded a few steps as Mike got closer to the beautiful casket and began speaking to his mother. "Mama I know I'm responsible for this. I've caused you nothing but stress and pain since the day I was born. I've broken your heart over and over again, no wonder it finally decided to give out on you. I have to live with knowing that, but I ask that you please forgive me. I love you," he said touching the casket, looking back over his shoulder at the men standing behind him. He then looked back at the casket one last time just as a single tear began rolling down his face. The tear shed wasn't in sadness but in shame at the thought of what he had become. As a child his mother had always hoped he would grow up to be a lawyer or even a baseball player but instead he had become a money hungry tyrant with a voracious appetite for power and blood. The thought of unfulfilled promises caused a few more tears to trickle down his face and land on top of the casket. The remorse disappeared as suddenly as it had arose and he quickly wiped the tears away. Who was he kidding; he loved his position as an apex predator atop of the criminal food chain. Even in the midst of war he still controlled the bulk of drugs and illegal activity in and around the Tri-State area and refused to cut any of the other families in. In fact, he was willing to do anything if it meant remaining in power. Even using the police to do his dirty work, providing information to put his competition out of business. A deplorable act, but his addiction to power had become stronger than his morals and respect for the rules of the underworld.

As Mike turned to walk towards the seats his men had cleared, the top of the casket suddenly flew open and a gunman with a black bandana covering everything on his face except his eyes popped up holding a Tec-9 and without warning began spraying everything in sight. Mike didn't stand a chance as the bullets began entering his back one after the other causing him to drop instantly. The two men closest to Mike were caught off guard as well and were killed before being able to reach for their weapons as shots struck them in their heads, snapping their necks back and dropping them. Chaos ensued and screams rang out as mourners in attendance scrambled frantically trying to find cover from the hail of bullets, while others hit the ground trying to avoid catching a stray. The remaining henchmen drew their weapons and began returning fire at the man as he leaped from the casket while still shooting. As the gunfire intensified two men dressed as groundskeepers pulled a pair of AR-15s out of trash cans and joined in, leaving the mobsters outgunned and unprepared for such an ambush. Bullets began ripping through the group, mowing them down like blades of grass.

When the gunfire ceased every man that had escorted Di Toro laid dead. Mike however was still clinging to life as he slowly crawled on his stomach a bloody mess. The gunmen who had sprung from the casket stood over him replacing his clip with a new one before using his foot to turn Mike over on to his back. Staring down at the supercilious gangster begging for his life to be spared made the masked man chuckle a bit.

"Not so tough now, huh champ," he said sarcastically, then squeezed the trigger emptying his clip into Mike's body and head.

CHAPTER 1

One Year Earlier

FBI- New York Field Office

"Good morning," Assistant Director Robert McCarthy's booming voice greeted the other agents seated throughout the large conference room. As leader of the Bureau's largest field office, McCarthy oversaw all operations and personnel in and around the five boroughs of New York City. "I first met with you late last year. We were all still coming to grips with the effects from Hurricane Sandy. Since that time we in the FBI have seen a dramatic boost in criminal threats. This morning I want to focus on one such threat, that of organized crime. Criminal syndicates in this city continue to con, extort and intimidate; just last week we arrested nearly 100 members from various families in New York and New Jersey but no one of significance. I'm tired of playing this game of cat and mouse. I want La Cosa Nostra brought to its knees," he fumed banging his hand on the table for emphasis.

The agents around the conference table remained silent; no one dared to interrupt his rant.

"Bring in Special Agent Mosley," he instructed the baby face agent seated in a chair against the wall.

The agent jumped from his seat and walked out the door before quickly returning, followed by a black man in his late 40's, who due to the rigorous demands of his job hadn't aged well, evident by his head full of grays.

"Agents, this is Special Agent Roosevelt Mosley, director of the new special task force I've created whose sole purpose will be to bring down organized crime in this city."

Special Agent Mosely exchanged greetings with the men and women in the room before taking a seat at the table and motioning for one of the young agents to hit the lights. He hit the clicker turning on the projector.

"Good morning agents. Every year organized crime drains millions of dollars of our national wealth, affecting legitimate businesses, labor unions and even sports. But most think of the mafia as part of America's past, its modern role merely the subject of popular television dramas. This is not the Sopranos with six guys sitting in a diner, shaking down a local business owner. These criminal enterprises are making millions of dollars through drug and human trafficking," he informed the group. "These are the five major crime families in the city," he said as their pictures appeared on the screen for all to see. "The Brigandi, Perrucci, Catanzano, Lucarelli and Martello families. These five families have dominated organized crime in the state of New York for decades, but it has come to our attention that this man," he said clicking the button switching the picture on the screen. "Marion Holloway is perhaps the most powerful gangster in the entire city."

Agent Jonathan Keaton slowly raised his hand. "Marion Holloway, the business man?"

"Yes," Special Agent Mosley answered.

Agent Keaton could not contain his amusement, "He is definitely a sly and ruthless business man. I mean he owns a cement company whose large trucks tear up our city streets and highways, then he have the contracts from the city to fix all the roads. Fucking genius," the agent admired. "I wouldn't say he's as a gangster. Hell he's never even been arrested for Christ sakes."

"Exactly," Mosley concurred. "That's because he knows who and what to target, and how to do it best. He is a capitalist and an entrepreneur but he is also a master criminal who moves undetected between the licit and illicit worlds. Marion runs his illegal businesses the same way he does his legal ones."

"Marion has insulated himself very well. Those in the

illegal side of his business never even interact with him. He's never around drugs or any violent acts," Director McCarthy chimed in.

"Well if he's so smart and has gone this long without being caught, what makes you so sure we can catch him now?" Agent Susan Gallagher asked.

The grumblings in the room grew louder as the agents began talking to one another. Most felt Mosley was overhyping the magnitude of Holloway's involvement in illegal activities. After all, how could someone get to the point where their power and influence rivaled the Italian mob and go unnoticed. Those that had heard of him only knew good things. He was a wildly successful business man, the leader of a prestigious family who did tons of work in the community and he and his wife were fixtures on the charity circuit. Mosley's claims seemed far-fetched.

"If you want to be reassigned that's fine with me," Mosley declared after seeing the skeptical looks on the faces in the room. "But if you want to be part of this task force, you got to be willing to follow my lead."

He paused to allow his message sink in. After he was sure he had the full attention of the room he rose from his seat and begin placing folders in front of every man at the table.

"Inside these folders you'll find everything you need to know about Marion and his team of players. Now I've been watching him for years and he's become lax as of late, allowing me to finally find a chink in his armor. One that I feel we can exploit if done properly."

Mosley stood quietly as the agents read through the pages inside the folders. He could see the doubt on their faces slowly begin to disappear with every flip of the page. He had been chasing Marion Holloway for years. They had history and now he finally had another opportunity to slap cuffs on him, one he didn't want to let get away.

"Ok agents listen," Assistant Director McCarthy's large voice startled the group as it seemed to shake the quiet room. "This is a very important operation but it is also very dangerous. We are dealing with men who kill with no hesitation or remorse. We've had more than a few CI's go missing trying to crack his organization. I urge that you use caution when coming in contact with any member of any of these organizations and I wish you all good luck."

* * *

The slight breeze coming off the waters of the Atlantic Ocean was just enough to compliment what had been another beautiful spring day. The sun shining off the blue water provided the perfect backdrop for the joyous occasion. The backyard of the massive estate in the East Hamptons had been transformed into a scene fit for royalty, New York City royalty. On this great day, the last Saturday in April, City Councilman Elijah Stokes had wed his fiancé. A statuesque beauty named

Cassandra Holloway. Thin but shapely, she looked so radiant dressed in her custom designed, white bridal gown that had been flown in from Paris only days before. Her smile seeming to grow with every congratulatory greeting she received from guests. Most were followed by white envelopes stuffed with various amounts of cash that she kept sticking into a white silk bridal bag that hung from her shoulder.

Elijah was a handsome groom. His freshly shaved bald head, neatly manicured goatee and milk chocolate skin blended perfectly with the reverse tuxedo look he had chosen for the occasion. He basked in the adoring eyes of his new wife, looking her way every few seconds to offer another smile. All while keeping a close eye on the money bag she was carrying. Watching the bulge in the bag grow, he smiled, thinking to himself how this was only the beginning. He had succeeded with the first step of his plan by marrying into the Holloway family, now he was ready to reap the benefits that came along with it. Not only the money but the boost it would give to his political career. One look at all the prominent figures scattered throughout the reception, he had no doubt about the direction he was heading in. In a world where who you know gets you into certain doors, his wife's father was the key to most of those locks.

Cassie, as she was called, truly loved Elijah. She had been through her share of heartache and to her he was heaven sent. He immediately connected with her two young sons and slowly became a father figure to them, something she found extremely attractive in him especially since he had no children of his own. For all her beauty she had twice the smarts, graduating from Princeton University magna cum laude. Cassie was an accountant by trade but more importantly she was the eldest daughter of the shrewd and powerful head of a lucrative business empire.

Marion Holloway was a well-respected man that many in the black community went to seeking help, and rarely were they turned away. He treated every man fair and everyone equal, rich or poor, powerful or weak. It was in his nature and it was how he raised his children to be. Through his relationships with the Italian Mafia, he operated an extensive heroin and cocaine trafficking network that covered over 15 states. Marion had slowly become one of the most influential men in the state and was viewed by those who knew as the most powerful black gangster in the country. He had his hands in a little bit of everything from politics and real estate to murder and money laundering. People in high ranking places owed him favors and he had his share of elected officials in his pocket and not just the black ones. That's because those pockets were as deep as the waters surrounding his beautiful vacation home, affording him the ability to do almost anything he wanted.

The extravagant wedding reception served as the perfect cover for the real reason he had summoned some of the city's decision makers and criminals to his home. Some had been afraid to attend not wanting to flaunt their relationship with him so publicly, while others didn't want to be paraded in front of the cameras of the federal agents that were sure to be camped outside taking pictures and writing down license plate numbers. Marion eased their fears by reminding his political guests that he had never been charged with any crimes, while informing the others to only come in vehicles that weren't registered to them.

Inside his office, in a secluded corner of the home, surrounded by a few politicians and the closest members of his organization, seated at the head of a large oak table was a strikingly handsome African American male, who despite being in his mid-fifties bore no resemblance to a man ready to collect on his pension. Tall, solid and fit as a man decades younger, the gray hairs in his salt and pepper goatee were the only signs of his true age.

Marion Holloway was born and bred in the streets of New York City, first in Harlem then in the Bedford Stuyvesant section of Brooklyn. His mother died when he was 6 years old and he was raised by his father, who owned a pool hall that was a hotspot for local hustlers, pimps and prostitutes in the 70's. He was a feared and respected presence in the underworld, a veteran combatant and known gunslinger with an exalted aura. Standing just under 6'3, with broad shoulders he was an imposing figure. When in his presence it was important to answer his questions directly and carry out his orders without hesitation. He had softened some over the years, preferring to use his astute business etiquette when getting things done. He still had an iron fist, only now it was covered in a velvet glove.

"So Marion what do we owe the pleasure?" slurred the middle aged white man slumped in a chair a few seats to the left, clearly feeling the effects of the unlimited amount of alcohol being served at the reception. He looked around the room for someone to cosign his line of questioning but found no willing participant.

"Still can't hold your liquor I see, Senator," Marion spoke calmly. "Pull yourself together it's embarrassing. It would be unfortunate for you to have a drunken mishap on your way home. Now wouldn't it?" Marion said sending a not so subtle threat and a look to match causing the man to sit up in his chair. "I appreciate everyone coming out to celebrate my daughter's wedding," he continued as a smile crept across his face. The normally stoic Marion was in great spirits after watching his first born daughter exchange nuptials. "But of course there is another reason I asked you all to be here," he said, now that he had the attention of the entire room. "I'm sure you're all aware that my son Mason has officially announced his candidacy for mayor of this wonderful city of ours. And as a favor to me, I'm asking for your support in making it a successful one." He informed them before getting up from his seat and walking around the table, stopping behind the chair of the drunken senator and putting his hand on his shoulder. "I know I can count on all of you in this room to help make that happen."

Most felt Mason was merely his father's puppet and had only advanced in his career due to the power and influence Marion possessed. No one in the room thought he was equipped to be the next mayor but they also knew Marion wasn't a man you said no to. When he asked for a favor he really wasn't asking. Also with Mason in office, anyone in good standings with his father could parlay that relationship into getting anything they needed done around the city. Everybody wanted to line their pockets with state and city funds and Marion knew it and used their greed to his advantage.

"Do you know what you're asking?" Harold Thompkins, a member of the House of Representatives that represented Brooklyn asked. "There has only been one black mayor in the city's history."

"Exactly, it's long overdue for another." Marion declared, "As a minority I thought you'd agree."

"I do," responded Thompkins, "I'm just not sure if..."

"Not sure if what?" Marion asked leaning forward in the man's face waiting for a response.

"If others will see it the same way," he said switching his original thoughts, not wanting to offend Marion by saying he thought Mason wasn't cut out to be mayor.

"I think I've built enough goodwill over the years to ask for some favors. You let me worry about that," Marion stated. "You just do your part," he informed the man.

"So you want us to rig the votes?" one person at the table questioned.

"No," Marion said laughing slightly, "But I do want you to influence voters."

"And how do you suggest we do that?" another person asked.

"I prefer the power of persuasion, but how you wield your influence is on you, just make it happen." Marion demanded. "I've seen a few of the preliminary polls and the numbers are not to my liking, so I need you on this like yesterday."

"Ok, let's say you pull it off, what's in it for us?" Carlos Mendez, the city's district attorney questioned.

"Leave it to the lawyer in the room to have his hand out," Marion said continuing to circle the table, fully prepared to deal with the slick talking lawyer. "You're coming up for re-election soon, correct?" Marion asked.

"Yes," he replied.

"Campaigns are costly, and scandal is a candidate's worst enemy. Watching all that money go to waste would be painful." He paused shaking his head back and forth. "But losing a career that has so much promise, now that would be a shame."

"Scandal?" the confused man questioned. "What are you talking about?" unaware of the can of worms he had just opened.

"What about the sexual harassment allegations from the tons of male assistants you've run through in the past few years?"

"Huh, what do you mean? There are no such allegations," he insisted. "I'm happily married, I'm not...gay," he said laughing nervously.

"Are you sure?" he asked staring the man down, letting him know he not only knew his secret but had already spoken to the victims that Mendez had paid off under the table, not to mention the male prostitutes he indulged in from time to time. "Wouldn't want that type of information getting out to the public, now would we, Mr. Mendez?"

The attorney just lowered his head in silence as the rest of the room prayed that their dirty laundry wouldn't be the next one coming out of his bag.

"So can I count on your votes?" Marion asked rhetorically, walking back to his chair and taking a seat. He had tons of dirt on every person in the room; it served as a reminder to them that his tentacles stretched far and wide and that none of them were untouchable. Displays of brute force was not his style, it was mental with him. He painted you into a corner until his way was your only option. "Now if you're not a member of my organization you're free to go."

* * *

"I'm really happy for you Cassie, Elijah is a good man," Mason said as he danced with his sister. "Now you have to give that man a baby of his own," he said referring to the fact she already had children before meeting her new husband. Mason was notorious for cruel comments like that, always reminding others of their flaws. He had always carried himself with an "*I'm better than you*" type of attitude, even amongst his siblings. He felt being the oldest made him right all the time.

"Yeah he is," she said unable to hide the smile that had been on her face since the wedding. Not even her brother's insensitive remarks could ruin her day. Elijah was the man of her dreams, tall, fine, smart and chocolate. He had swept her off her feet and she hadn't touched the ground since. They had met through Mason almost two years ago and their wedding was the culmination of a whirlwind love affair. Mason took pride in knowing that he was partly responsible for his sister's happiness whether she acknowledged it or not.

"You mind if I cut in?" said a voice from over Mason's shoulder.

"Sin!" Cassie screamed letting her brother know exactly who it was standing behind him, leaving him no need to turn around.

"No problem," Mason said as his smile slowly disappeared hearing the excitement in her voice. He stepped aside without making eye contact with the intruder before making his way over to the table occupied by his mother and younger sister.

"Damn Cassie, you look so beautiful, but you always look beautiful," Sin charmed as he replaced Mason, seamlessly falling into rhythm with the gorgeous bride. "So what's better than beautiful?"

"Stunning, exquisite," she replied as she stepped back allowing him to take all of her in, still beaming unable to hide her excitement.

"All of the above. I'm real happy for you," he said in his smooth baritone voice. "I got something for you." He informed her reaching inside his suit pulling out a thick white envelope handing it to her, then kissing her on the cheek before stopping her from placing it in the bridal bag. "That's just for you. I'm sure you know what to do with it."

"What is he doing here?" Emma Holloway, the fiery matriarch of the family said to her son Mason as he sat down next to her. Like a fine wine Emma's undeniable beauty only seemed to better with age. Her golden complexion, long silky black hair and full lips were a perfectly blended representation of her Afro-Cuban decent. Her model like figure hadn't changed much over the years, even after four kids, evident by the way she looked astonishing in her blue, off the shoulder dress. A fixture in high society, she liked to fancy herself as somewhat of a philanthropist, attending charitable functions and contributing generously to many causes. But the truth was she only did it because she knew it made her look good. Frankly, she could care less about those less fortunate than her. She just wanted to be the one cutting the biggest check at the event, so all the other women would have something to talk about.

"Who knows, but I'm sure Pops invited him," Mason said clearly unhappy about Sin's presence.

"Your father and his charity case," Emma said exhaling a deep breath.

"Why wouldn't Sin be here?" the younger sister, Ashleigh, chimed in on her mother and brother's discussion. "He's our brother."

"Brother, Tsssk! Yasin Kennedy is not your brother my dear, he's your father's mistake. Ghetto trash just like the whore he came out of." Emma spewed her venomous words before sipping her champagne.

"Ma," Ashleigh shouted showing her displeasure at her mother's statement. "That woman is dead."

"And it serves her right," Emma continued while twisting up her face, unfazed by her daughter's disapproval. She had never hid her feelings towards her husband's bastard child or his deceased mother and wasn't about to start now. She had long forgiven Marion for the affair that resulted in Sin's birth, but she never accepted him. Her hatred for him only seemed to grow stronger the more he grew into the splitting image of her husband. Sin not only resembled his father more than any of the other children, he also possessed his charm and all of his mannerisms. That really ate at Emma. Although her children had been afforded all the luxuries of living in exclusive neighborhoods, attending private schools and receiving the best education money could buy. It was clear by the way Sin's mere presence commanded a room, that the leadership trait had skipped her eldest son. The one she hoped would eventually reach the highest level of political success.

Mason Holloway, the oldest of the Holloway children, was a 35 year old who looked the part of the city's next mayor. He was golden brown like his mother, with high cheekbones and almond shaped eyes. His good grade of hair was cut low and even all the way around and was slightly receding in the front. Normally sporting a beard or goatee, he had recently gone clean shaven in order to appear more suited for the mayor's office. In his mind he was on the fast track to the Governor's Mansion and maybe beyond.

Idolizing his father's stature since a child, Mason wanted nothing more than to follow in his powerful footsteps. Though he tried his best, in most instances, those footprints had always proved too large to fill. Marion's dream for his son had always been for him to go into politics. He pushed all his children into legal occupations, hoping to build generations of Holloways that were looked at like the Kennedys. Mason was to be the first pillar in that structure and he used all his resources to make sure he would be a success. To the naked eye he was, but behind his back there were snickers that he was nothing more than his father's invention, an under qualified candidate with powerful backing. There was a bit of truth to the murmurs, Marion connections had gotten his son further than most. He had also spearheaded most of his campaigns, even coming up with the ideas and policies he had run on in his previous victories in lower offices in the city.

While Mason coveted his father's power and influence, it was Emma who had the most influence on him. Mason was his mother's pride and joy, her first born child who aimed to do nothing but please her. Emma knew it and she used it to her advantage, constantly dropping seeds in his mind then watering them over time allowing them to bloom into ideas he thought were his own. Even his choice of bride had been influenced heavily by her, all with his future aspiration in mind. Mason had truly been groomed for the world of high stake politics.

He sat staring at his sister dancing with Sin, until his wife, Khari; a cocoa skinned elegant beauty tapped him on the shoulder breaking his concentration.

"C'mon babe let's dance," she urged.

"I'm not really in the mood," he seethed seemingly annoyed by her request, his every thought consumed by his unwanted sibling's presence.

Situated at a separate table hoping to escape the malevolent tongue of his mother, sat another sibling, Josiah

Holloway, or Jewlz as he was called by in the family. The youngest of all the Holloway children, the handsome caramel toned, twenty-two-year-old was in his senior year at Yale where he was majoring in business. Marion had called on more than one favor getting him into the prestigious institute and had to use up a couple more keeping him there. Jewlz's grades never were an issue; he just couldn't avoid staying out of trouble. His good looks and his rebellious ways gave him an edge that appealed to most of the girls on campus, including the pretty young lady that had accompanied him to the wedding.

"I'll dance wit you," he interjected seeing the potential for an argument arising. "That's if you don't mind," he said turning to his date who quickly gave her approval.

"C'mon Jewlz," Khari said quickly accepting. "At least there are still some gentlemen left in this family," she fumed shooting her husband a dirty look as they passed him on their way to dance.

The two joined Sin and Cassie on the dance floor. "Looking good lil' bro," Sin said seeing his baby brother dancing next to him, dressed sharply.

Jewlz reached out dapping his sibling. His admiration for his brother boarded on worship, Sin moved like a boss, something Jewlz studied like one of his college textbooks and wanted more than anything. While everyone in the family pushed him to excel in school and help further the family's legitimate affairs, he dreamed of being involved in all aspects of his father's business, just like Sin. He didn't know exactly what that entailed and was smart enough not to ask a lot of questions. He just knew he wanted the same type of respect Sin had, the same respect he seen his father receive as well.

"Hey, can I have my wife back?" Elijah asked causing them all to laugh. His bride had been dancing with everyone else for long enough, he was ready to wrap his arms around her once again.

"No doubt, my bad," Sin said stepping back. "Congratulations bro, you got a good one right here," he said looking at his sister while reaching in his suit once again to retrieve a thick envelope and handing it to him. "Take care of my sister," he said leaning in for a pound and a tight embrace to emphasis the seriousness of his last statement.

"I plan on it," Elijah replied. "Thanks, by the way, Mr. Holloway wants to see you," he said pointing towards the house.

* * *

The orange flame lit the tip of the Montecristo as Marion took a pull and blew out a large cloud of smoke before sinking into the plush leather chair in his office. Seated directly across from him was Phil Catanzano, the portly Don of the crime family that bore his name. He controlled the docks on the west side of Manhattan and parts of New Jersey. He was a completely disarming man whose round face resembled a cake baker more than it did a mafia boss. His family dealt mostly in legitimate businesses including owning most of the bread and milk routes in the city. But his control of the waterfronts proved to be his most lucrative business, he was the key component in the drug smuggling operation of the other families. Of the Five Italian Families in the city, his was the least powerful but the most amiable. Along with the two men was Marion's second in command, Nate Walker, enjoying a celebratory cigar and drink with the father of the bride. Marion and Big Phil, as he was called, had done business together for many years and had developed a friendship over that period of time, so it was no surprise he had shown up to the wedding. But his request to talk business on a day like today was, but after hearing the urgency in Phil's voice Marion quickly agreed.

"First let me say I mean no disrespect asking to talk business on your daughter's wedding day and I truly apologize," Phil began. "But this was something that couldn't wait."

"C'mon Phil, you know better than that. No disrespect taken," a jovial Marion said tilting his glass of cognac towards Catanzano. "What's going on?"

"Carlo Brigandi is on his death bed and is not expected to live much longer." Phil said bringing the mood of the room down some. "His health is deteriorating at a rapid pace I'm being told, and he could pass away at any moment."

Marion didn't like hearing the news about the Don of the Brigandi family, not only was he the oldest and longest tendered Don in all the "Five Families" but he was also the man who Marion's father had worked under for many years and had made it possible for him to reach the levels of the game that he had out of pure love for his dad.

Marion looked over at Nate, who just shook his head in disbelief only able to offer up a single word. "Damn."

"So the old man is finally showing signs of his age?" Marion joked trying to lighten up the mood that had fallen upon the room. "I thought he would stay forever young," he continued.

"Yeah, me too." Phil confessed. "But here's the thing," he said sitting his glass down on the table in front of him. "For a long time now the old man has been the only thing holding the "Five Families" together. If he goes...all hell could break loose."

"Yeah?" Marion replied seemingly unfazed by the news.

"Yeah and I think Mike Di Toro is gearing up to make a power play for control." Phil proclaimed.

"Control of what?" Marion asked.

"Of the business and a bigger piece of territory."

"The families are all equal partners. No one controls more than their twenty percent worth."

"Yeah but word is that Di Toro has been dying to wage

war against the other families for a while now, but out of respect for Carlo he hasn't. With the old man gone, there is nothing stopping him." Phil suggested.

"Di Toro has always been a hot head with fortune and fame in his sights and schemes of grandeur on his mind." Marion declared. "But what does that have to do with me? I'm not part of the in crowd," he said eluding to the fact that he was not Italian and his organization was not part of the "Five Families."

"But when it rains everyone gets wet. If he succeeds, the war won't stop with us. You're the next biggest fish in the sea," Phil reminded him.

"Yeah, and I'd stand alone in war like I stand alone now." Marion stated confidently. "I respect you Phil but I can't drag my family into a war that has absolutely nothing to do with us, it's not good business. So for now I'm gonna sit this one out," Marion said firmly.

Catanzano just nodded his head and tilted his glass towards Marion before taking a sip. Though he disagreed with his friend's choice he still had to respect it. He too knew what a war would mean and could cost his family greatly. As a leader he hoped it wouldn't come to that, he thought it was bad for business. "Well let me get back out here to my wife," he said rocking back and forth before getting to his feet. He reached over and shook Marion's hand and said his congratulations once again before heading out the door.

Nate waited until he saw the door close behind the mobster then looked at Marion and asked, "Whatchu think about that? Di Toro is strong. If he decided to war it's not much those other families can do to stop him."

Marion nodded in agreement. "Yeah...but Phil is smart, something Di Toro isn't," he reminded his friend. "And he's strong enough."

* * *

Opening the door to his father's massive office, Sin found him like he had most times, locked in a debate with his oldest and closest friend. They were usually arguing over the details of a story from their past and today was no different.

"It was 72," Nate said in his normally loud and animated tone, trying to prove his point.

"It was 73, Nate," Marion stated calmly, confident in his recollection. "73."

Seeing his father was like looking in a mirror that showed the future. Their bronze skin and handsome features, including their wavy hair and thousand-watt smile, mirrored each other and was noticeable to anyone who saw them. While the elder Marion looked more distinguished and gentlemen like, Sin's look and swagger was a little more rugged and street but equally as handsome.

"Come here Sin," Nate said waving him over after seeing him enter the room. "Grab a seat young blood."

Filling the empty chair next to his father, Sin could see the two old friends were in a great mood. If the cloud of cigar smoke surrounding them wasn't enough, the smirks on their faces were a dead giveaway.

"Wassup Uncle Nate, what y'all old heads arguing about now?" Sin asked.

"Tell ya father, that the last time his sorry ass Knicks won the title was in 1972," Nate demanded.

"I told this ma'fucka they lost in the finals in 72. They won in 70 and 73," Marion said.

"Yeah...Pops is right Unc." Sin proclaimed.

"Aah, you'on know shit lil' nigga, you wasn't even born yet," Nate said laughing but still disagreeing.

"What's going on tho Pops? Elijah said you wanted to see me. What's good?"

"Life, youngster," Marion expressed blowing more smoke into the air. "Life is good."

"Yeah I guess so." Sin said with a smile leaning back in the chair.

"You see your sister out there? She's beautiful isn't she?" Marion beamed.

Sin nodded his head. "Yeah, I was just dancing wit' her before I came up." Cassie had always been his favorite out of all his siblings. She was the one he was closest to, not just in their relationship but in age also; they were only 10 months apart. So it warmed his heart seeing her so happy. "I saw

Catanzano on my way in. What's that about?" Sin asked switching gears.

"Carlo Brigandi is dying and when he does, Phil thinks the Martello family is gonna wage a war for control." Marion spoke in between puffs.

"Whatchu think?" Sin quizzed.

"Maybe," Marion said. "It's possible."

"I agree," Nate said knowing Sin was going ask the same question of him.

"So where we standing if it go down like that?" Sin inquired but already knowing his father's answer.

"On the sidelines," Marion insisted. "I gotta plan but for now we'll remain neutral," Marion answered.

"It's your call." Sin said nodding his head but seeming to disagree.

"We're in the money business, son," Marion informed his offspring. "And war is never good for business."

He knew Sin had his own ideas of what they should be doing and how they should be proceeding and Marion admired his inherited sense of leadership. He knew the day would come when Sin would be at the helm of the organization, but that time hadn't arrived yet. He also knew, like it or not, Sin would always follow his wishes. He was as solid as they came. Unlike his other children, Marion had never tried to sway Sin from the streets. He knew he would be just wasting his breath. The young man was cut from the same fabric he was; bred for the game more like him than either of them cared to admit. Everything about him screamed hustler, make a dollar and double it and to move anybody trying to interfere with that out of the way, always business never personal. Marion always had a different level of respect for Sin than any of his other children; he was always his own man. Even under his father's organization he still maintained and ran his own crew.

The sound of the door opening again grabbed their attention causing them to stop speaking and direct their eyes towards it. Mason slowly entered the room, unenthused by his brother's presence. The two siblings rarely spoke and did their best to avoid each other all together. They were on different ends of the same organization and most times one's actions directly affected the others but you would never know it by the way they acted towards each other. Mason, like his mother, believed Sin was an outsider. He wasn't a full-blooded Holloway, so he wasn't family. That was only the top layer of a more deep rooted hatred that centered around Marion's perceived favoritism towards his bastard child. Mason's blood boiled every time he thought about how his father showed so much trust in the street urchin. Mason believed he should be more involved in the illegal activities of his father's empire; after all he had sat at the feet of the king his entire life. He was the rightful heir; first born, full blooded.

"I didn't know you had company Pops," Mason said

sarcastically upon entering the room.

Company, Sin thought to himself causing him to let out a slight laugh. *This clown ass nigga here.*

"Come in here Mase," the elder Holloway said greeting his son. "I was just discussing a couple of things with your brother and uncle, including Sin helping get you into that big office in city hall." Marion said ignoring the tension between the two like he always did. His approach was to force them to work together, with the hopes that it would thaw their icy relationship. But so far it hadn't seemed to work.

"Help?" Mason quipped. "What could he possibly do for me? I don't need his help. Most of the people he knows can't vote anyway."

"You need all the help you can get," Sin said unable to contain himself as he rose to his feet and buttoned his suit jacket. "I got some business I need to go see about," he said while looking down at his phone before turning his attention back to his father. "I'll holla at you later Pops. Good seeing you again Uncle Nate," he said patting him on the back.

"You sure?" Marion asked. "We haven't made the toast yet. You have to say something," he pleaded.

"I'm sure Barack here can handle it," Sin cracked staring Mason up and down as he walked past him towards the door.

"Go ahead and get back to your homies and your corners, you don't belong here anyway." Mason snidely responded looking over his shoulder at Sin.

Most wouldn't dare speak to Sin that way and those that pressed their luck usually were left in need of pallbearers. But out of respect for his father he just laughed it off. "Me and my homies are the reason you're able to sleep peacefully at night. Remember that," he said just before closing the door behind him.

"Did you see the news about the preliminary polls?" Mason asked turning back towards his father and uncle after watching the door close. He was clearly feeling uneasy by the results which had him trailing. It was early but it still was a big deal, at least to him it was.

"Yeah, I saw it." Marion answered while putting his cigar out in the ashtray before standing up.

"That ain't shit Mase, you got this in the bag," Nate said.

"In the bag, Pops?" Mason asked trying to get a response that would indicate if his father was going all out for him behind the scenes to ensure his victory.

"What do you mean, have I ever let you down?" the elder questioned with a laugh. "Today's your sister's wedding day son," Marion said walking over to Mason placing his hands on his shoulders. "It's a joyous occasion. That's a subject for another time. Today we celebrate!" he said shaking him playfully. "Now let's get back outside before your mother comes looking for us."

* * *

Sin walked out the front door of the massive Holloway estate into the driveway filled with a plethora of luxury vehicles. A who's who of New York's elite society had shown up to witness the exchange of nuptials between Elijah and Cassie and the wealth was on full display in the driveway. Sin stood removing his tie while waiting for the valet to retrieve his car when his phone began to ring. Seeing the number he quickly answered it. "Yeah I know, I'm on my way now," was all he said before hanging up.

The valet had just pulled up when he noticed Khari coming up the driveway holding something in her hand. She had accidently left one of the newlyweds' gifts in her trunk and had rushed to her car to get it. Upon her return she was forced to hesitate briefly before continuing up the driveway, caught off guard by Sin's presence. She wanted to reverse her course, but decided to just walk by him and avoid making eye contact, a common thing between the two.

Sin walked around the front of his car and tipped the valet as he stood holding the door open before smoothly slipping into the driver's seat. He watched as Khari hastily strutted in front of his car and up the steps back into the estate just before pulling off.

CHAPTER 2

Harv pushed his black 745 BMW through the streets of Brooklyn bobbing his head to the sounds of Pusha T, a blunt filled with Cali's finest hanging from his lips. His Cartier frames sat on his light skinned face and his Yankee hat was tilted, giving a peek at the waves that spun on his freshly cut fade. The Jesus piece at the end of his chain rested on his chest and flickered as the passing street lights hit the diamonds he had engraved in the entire face. Pulling up to the curb and parking, Harv hit the button on his A/C, opening the secret stash spot in the dash where he kept his Beretta 9 mm. He retrieved the gun and chambered a round before tucking it in his waist and hopping out the car. Bopping up the walkway that led to the front of the building, he dapped up two of his workers seated on the benches as he passed. A third worker stood posted in front of the project building and greeted him with a handshake and hug before he entered the door.

Ascending the steps to the second floor apartment that housed the spot, he quickly made his way down the hallway. Approaching the door, Harv knocked twice before pausing then knocked five more times in rapid succession letting the crew inside know it was him. He had already called ahead letting them know he was coming through to make the daily pick up. He expected them to have it ready for him when he arrived, hoping to get in and out as quickly as possible. He was looking forward to hitting the strip club for some entertainment after dropping off the cash. Harv could hear footsteps approach the door then stop, just before hearing the door being unlocked. Just as the door was cracked the apartment door directly across the hall swung open and a group of masked men waving guns emerged and pushed Harv into the apartment.

* * *

The yellow crime scene tape covering the entrance of the apartment was all that needed to be seen for the neighbors on the second floor of the project building to begin gathering in the hallway and start speculating about what may have taken place inside of apartment 2H. That was the scene when Wilfredo Alvarado and Malik Harris stepped off the elevator into the mob forming in the hallway. The two hot shot detectives both been on the force for 7 years and had been partners for the last 5 of them. Making their way up the hallway they passed some uniformed officers before being stopped by one of them at the door of the apartment. Both men pulled their badges that they had hooked to gold chains around their necks from inside their shirts before proceeding under the yellow tape into the apartment.

Upon entering they immediately saw three bodies laid out in the front room on the floor side by side covered in white sheets. Alvarado kneeled down next to one of the bodies and pulled back the sheet.

"Got damn," he said looking up at his partner. "This is a fucking kid," he said shaking his head.

"He don't look no older than 18 or 19," Det. Harris said looking down at the body of the young man his partner had peeled the sheet off of. "It's a cold and heartless game."

"Cold as fuck." Det. Alvarado agreed. "This is the fourth one of these we've seen in the past two months," he said rising to his feet. "All drug spots, no witnesses, no survivors."

"So, we gotta group of vigilantes out here taking out drug dealers," Harris said as a smile crept across his face. "That's not so bad when you think about it," he declared with a laugh.

Alvarado found humor in it as well as he laughed at his partner's comments. "They said it's another body in the back room," he told Harris before heading down the hallway of the two bedroom apartment into the back bedroom with his partner right behind him. As they entered the room the crime scene investigators were getting forensics off of a body that was laid out on the floor in front of an open safe. The body was face down and the victim looked to have been shot execution style. The two detectives approached just as the coroner was turning the corpse over allowing the men to get a good look at the deceased man.

"Isn't that Harv?" Harris said recognizing the victim first and leaning down to get a closer look.

"Yup, sure is," Alvarado responded. "Isn't he part of your boy Sin's crew?"

"Yeah," Harris said. "So this has to be one of his spots." The detective concluded.

"Who in Brooklyn has the balls to rob one of his spots?" Alvarado wondered aloud.

"Whoever it is, better pray we find em before he does." Harris said bluntly.

* * *

Traffic slowly cruised past the flashing lights of the NYPD patrol cars parked in front of the building where the quadruple homicide had taken place. Sin blended in with the slow flow of cars and surveyed the scene outside the project building taking mental notes of the faces that were out there, especially the ones being interviewed by police. Sin had circled the block a few times and was satisfied that he had seen enough. He turned the corner making a left on Thompkins Ave, then a right on Myrtle Ave headed towards the Marcy Projects.

Pulling up to the curb, Sin hopped out of the car joined by his right hand man, Sean Boston or Beans as everybody called him. The two men had been best friends dating back to their childhood days growing up in Fort Green Projects in Brooklyn. They shared an unbreakable bond and were extremely loyal to one another. For years they had run the streets being the eyes behind each other's back. While Sin was a strategic thinker, only making calculated moves, Beans was more of a hot head and acted on impulses. They seemed like polar opposites but it was their differences that made their friendship work, they provided balance for each other. Sin trusted Beans more than anyone. He knew his friend would lay down his life for him and he would do the same in return. Long before he knew about his Holloway ties, Beans was his brother and that hadn't changed. Once he was offered a position in his father's organization, he brought his man in to watch his back. Beans had a deep hatred for the Italians and wasn't too fond of having to do business with them. He would much rather kill them all. But that was Beans he would rather just kill anybody he didn't like. He enjoyed that part of the game, along with all the money that came with it and left the politics of the drug game to Sin.

Waiting on the two men, standing inside the gates of the basketball courts, were top members of Sin's crew were Barkim and Ali; two brothers from Marcy and Sheik, a stocky built dark skinned cat with a neatly groomed beard that made him resemble the Aks from Philly. They had been running with Sin and Beans since their high school days and were all battle tested soldiers on the streets. Standing with them was Kyrie, a young gunner that Sin had taken under his wing years ago. Being groomed by a nigga with Sin's pedigree gave the youngin' a leg up on niggas his age. He was a thoroughbred who was never unprepared, always strapped and trained to go. Although he was the youngest in the crew he had put in his share of work earning him the respect of every member. His curly hair, light complexion and baby face made him appear younger than he was but if you underestimated him you wouldn't live to regret it. The sleeves on his black shirt were rolled up giving a glimpse of the tattoos that covered both arms completely. His crisp black jeans and jordans matched perfectly with his Brooklyn Nets snapback that he wore backwards. He was the first to greet the men with pounds and hugs.

"Yo what the fuck is goin' on?" a clearly upset Sin asked while clapping his hands together for emphasis. "Niggas runnin' up in our spots now? That should never happen. Everybody out here know how we play or at least they supposed to," he said scanning back and forth looking into the eyes of all the men. "Y'all niggas out here slippin? How dis happen?"

"I can't even lie my nigga, I don't know." Ali, the younger

of the two brothers answered honestly.

"You gotta do better than that my G," a frustrated Sin demanded.

"Yo, word on the block is it's some niggas out here hitting spots all over the city. They hit a few spots last month but it wasn't on my radar like that 'cuz I didn't think niggas was dumb enough to come at us," Barkim, the older and slightly darker of the two brothers informed Sin.

"When the last time you put some work in?" Sin questioned. "Niggas can't be out here living off they rep, thinking one of these new niggas won't try you."

"It gotta be some outta town niggas who don't know no better Sin. I can't see no local niggas that fucking stupid," Beans said dying for the chance to find the people responsible.

"I know what tho, when we do find out who it was them niggas is food. Harv was my nigga." Ali answered.

"I feel you. Harv was my guy too plus he had just put my lil' nigga on at the spot," he said lowering his head saddened by thought. "Lil' nigga was only 17 but he was as solid as they come," Sheik said.

"Yeah I fucked wit son like that too," Kyrie admitted.

"Yo I want this shit taken care of ASAP. Got us looking crazy out here right now. Can't give these niggas no ideas, ya feel me?" Sin explained. "I need y'all wit ya ears to the street finding out who dee'z niggas are. Ain't nobody ever take shit from me but a bullet or ass whipping and I ain't about to start letting it happen now. I want them niggas dead before our people go in the ground."

"No doubt," Barkim agreed.

"Yo Ali, get word to Harv's peoples that I'ma cover all his funeral expenses. Nigga was a good dude. He deserved to be sent out the right way," Sin said.

"What about the youngin'?" Sheik asked.

"Same thing." Sin said before dapping everybody up and heading back to his car.

CHAPTER 3

Emma sat at her vanity stroking the brush through her hair slowly as she stared at herself in the mirror. Finally allowing her hair to lay on her shoulder, she ran her fingers through it a couple more times. It had been a long day, but a day any mother would have been proud of. Seeing a daughter get married should have been a highlight of motherhood. But for Emma, Sin's appearance at the reception was all she could think about. She knew her husband was up to something. It was figuring out what that had her mind racing. She knew he was grooming Sin to one day take over his criminal enterprise but she felt his focus should be more on helping Mason become mayor and like with all things she wasn't going to hold her tongue.

Marion exited the bathroom into the oversized master bedroom and headed straight for the closet. Truthfully, there wasn't anything he needed in there. He had seen the familiar scowl on Emma's face and knew she wanted to talk. The trip into the closet was his way of delaying the inevitable. Upon his exit Emma wasted no time digging for information.

"So what was Yasin doing here today?" she asked getting straight to what it was that she wanted to know. Rarely did she beat around the bush with anyone including Marion. It was one of the things that had attracted him to her many years ago. Her straight forwardness mixed with her passionate intensity when it came to her family still turned him on all these years later. Emma had a lioness like protection over her family and wasn't going to see anyone she deemed unworthy benefit off of what she felt rightfully belonged to her children, mainly Mason. Sin threatened the order of succession, so he was the enemy.

"The same thing everyone else was doing here, Emma," he answered already aware of where the conversation was going. He had fielded her complaints about his son for years and had long grown tired of them. "For Cassie and Elijah."

"Oh really, he seemed more interested in what you had going on, on the inside of the house," she said.

"What makes you say that?" he questioned.

"He didn't stay long, in and out. I thought that was rude. But what else should I have expected? He was raised by a whore. Getting in and out quickly is in his blood."

Marion just shook his head. "He would have loved to stay longer but had to take care of some business." He informed her.

"What kind of business?" she inquired.

"His business." He stated sternly letting it be known he wasn't feeling her line of questioning and she was toeing the line.

"Well, I think you've been focusing on his business a little too much," she said using her hands to assign quotation. "Instead you should be focusing more on Mason and his campaign. I've seen the preliminary polls and they are not favorable numbers. This is a big moment for this family Marion, this means the world to Mason and he needs you. He needs your expertise but most importantly he needs your undivided attention."

"First of all, never tell me what I should be doing. Secondly, I got everything under control. Don't I always?" he asked rhetorically. "Don't worry your pretty little head," he said now standing behind her before leaning over and kissing her on the top of her head. "I'm going to bed."

Emma sat staring at her reflection in the mirror again. Marion was right, he had always kept things under control but those things meant nothing to her. Mason becoming mayor meant everything to her and she needed her husband to feel the exact same way. They had been building towards this moment for years and now that it was finally upon them she wasn't going let it slip through her family's fingers. No one, including her husband, was going screw it up especially not

Keys to the Kingdom
over Sin.

CHAPTER 4

Sin turned his smoke grey 6 series onto 11th Avenue and parked in front of Manhattan Motorcars, the luxury car dealership he had purchased over a year ago, located between W. 28th & W.27th Street. Growing up he always had a fetish for cars, so owning a dealership seemed like the natural thing to do. He didn't hesitate once his sister Cassie presented him with the opportunity. The former owner had gotten himself in a financial squeeze and needed to sell the company. Sin was more than happy to take it off his hands at a well undervalued price. The thriving business, located in a prime spot on the west side, doubled as his headquarters and served as the perfect cover for all his illegal activities. Most employees were members of his crew whom he had taught the business, allowing him the ability to schedule drop offs and pick-ups, as well as conduct business meetings during test drives. It was an intricate network he had in place but it had proven to be a very lucrative one.

Entering the doors of the dealership with Beans right behind him, Sin quickly made his way through the showroom passing BMW's, Benz's, Audi's, Porsche's and Range Rovers . He immediately stopped in his tracks after catching a glimpse of the new red Ferrari 458 parked in the middle of the showroom floor.

"That ma'fucka bad right?" he asked his partner tapping him and pointing.

"Hell yeah," Beans replied at the sight of the immaculate vehicle.

Sin made a mental note to himself to get a closer look at the new vehicle a little later, which would definitely include a test drive. But for now he had business in his office he needed to take care of with Beans.

"Close those blinds my nigga," he instructed Beans as they entered the office and closed the door behind them. Sin walked over to the safe in the wall and punched in the code. He opened the safe revealing two bricks of cocaine. Removing them, he placed them on the desk. "Look at this shit my nigga," he said clearly disgusted. "I been seeing this shit a lot lately, it's a few with every shipment it seems like," he continued, pointing at the two white bricks laying there.

Beans moved in closer getting a better look and could clearly see that the bricks had been played in. The middle of each one had been scooped out a little, not enough to alarm the naked eye, but enough for a person to make a nice profit if done to several bricks a shipment. "I saw a few of dem shits too," he declared.

"I'on put shit past a mu'fucka, but I know they ain't coming like that. The cubans ain't trying to fuck up the type of money they making with us," he said sitting in the chair and leaning back. "Nah this got the nigga City written all over it. I been on to his shit for a minute. Get rid of that nigga. I don't wanna see him no more. Then let youngin' and the twins take over his spot."

"Say no more my nigga, I'm on it," Beans said eager for the opportunity to make an example out of someone.

"On another note tho, what's the word on dem niggas that ran up in our shit?" Sin asked switching subjects.

"Still nothing."

"Put some mo' money on they head, somebody know who they is. I want them niggas dealt wit'," Sin explained. "Niggas out here stealing from me left and right," Sin said while picking one of the bricks up off the desk waving it up and down. "I should start giving this shit away for free if we gonna make it that easy." His frustration was evident.

"I feel you. Like I said I'm on it." Beans reassured his friend. "And this other shit too," he said pointing at the bricks on the desk as he rose to his feet. "But I'm 'bout to slide to the club."

"This early?" Sin asked looking at his watch.

"It's Friday my nigga. It's our biggest night. Gotta make sure ay'thing straight."

"Aight," Sin said dapping his man up.

Sin rose to his feet just as Beans closed the door. He picked the work up off the desk, walked back over to the safe and placed it back inside before locking it away. Sin then strolled over and opened the blinds of the office windows, allowing him to look out into the showroom floor. Thoughts of taking that new Ferrari for a spin re-entered his mind and he decided to head out of the office in search of the keys.

He located the sales floor manager, but before he could ask for the keys he noticed he was speaking with a customer. Moving closer, Sin was able to get a better look at the woman and was immediately captivated by her beauty. Overhearing their conversation, he learned she was looking to test drive a few vehicles before making a purchase.

"I'm sorry ma'am, but we do test drives by appointment only," the manager informed her. "But I can see if any sales reps are available to schedule you an appointment," he said as he looked around for someone to assist the woman but came up empty, as they all seemed to be busy with customers. "Umm, if you don't mind waiting I can have somebody with you in just a few."

"I can help her," Sin said seizing the opportunity. "I don't have any customers." He continued by putting his hand on the manager's shoulder. To the man's surprise he turned to see his boss standing next to him. Confused by the offer, he gave Sin a look to which the boss replied. "I don't mind." Sin extended his hand. "Hello Miss, I'm Yasin, I'll be the sales rep helping you today," he said flashing a smile. The woman smiled back delighted at the handsome man standing in front of her offering to help.

The manager quickly caught on and left the two alone.

"Anything in particular that you're interested in?" Sin asked noticing she too had eyes for the red Ferrari.

"No not really, I'm open. Any suggestions?" she asked.

"What price range are you trying to stay in?" he asked.

"Money's not an issue," she replied.

Sin laughed to himself digging her style. "Ok, I got something you might like. Let me go get the keys," he said before disappearing in the back.

Sin returned with a key belonging to an all-white Porsche Panamera. The look she gave him displayed her approval as he pointed out the car to her. He handed her the keys. "Let's ride," he said while opening the passenger side door.

They pulled onto 11th and made a quick right on W. 27th before turning onto 12th Ave. heading towards 42nd St. Sin relaxed in the passenger's seat admiring how good the driver looked behind the wheel guiding them through the city. She was gorgeous, even more mesmerizing up close. Her blemish free golden brown skin gave no indication of her age and her chinky eyes hinted at her being mixed with something other than black. The woman's long black hair flowed to the middle of her back with soft curls. Her perfectly arched eyebrows and full lips made her beauty undeniable. She calmly glided through traffic, seemingly made for the sports car and enjoying the ride.

"So whatchu think?" Sin asked.

"I like it," she quickly replied. "The ride is smooth."

"You look good...behind the wheel," he said wanting to flirt after giving her hands a look and not seeing a ring. "I'm sorry I didn't get your name," he realized.

"How rude of me, I apologize. I'm Ariane," she stated, finally giving him a name to match her intoxicating smile.

Ariane, he thought to himself. *I like that,* he thought as he stored it in his memory. "Can you see yourself owning one of these?"

"Maybe," she replied.

"Maybe? What's holding you back from saying yes? It's a beautiful car. You should treat yourself." Sin insisted.

"You're absolutely right, but you can't jump at the first thing you see. Majority of the time you end up disappointed. I like to take my time," she answered.

Sin just nodded in agreement, having no choice but to respect her answer. "I definitely want you to be pleased, so would you like to head back and test drive something else?"

"You're really trying to sell me a car today aren't you?" she joked sarcastically.

"Or spend more time with you, it just depends on how you look at it," he said flashing a smile she was quickly becoming drawn to.

"Stalker," she joked.

Sin didn't laugh though something else had diverted his attention. He noticed the same grey Malibu two cars back had been following them since they had pulled out of the dealership. He had been watching the car the entire time. The two white male passengers both sported sunglasses and were doing their best to remain close to the Porsche.

"Is everything alright?" she asked. "I was just joking," she assured him noticing he hadn't laughed at all.

"No everything is cool," he said calmly. "I was just thinking of another car you might like. Let's get back before they start thinking you kidnapped me," he said joking back to soothe her uneasiness after her statement.

Sin's mind began to fill with thoughts of who they could be. He knew it wasn't the local detectives because he knew most of their faces, so he immediately thought they were the feds. But seeing the way the men were trying to stay close as possible and had even attempted to speed up to get on the side of their car a few times, he began to question whether or not they were cops at all. The talk he had with his father at the wedding played back in his mind. *Damn that could be some of Di Toro's people.* Unsure of a definitive answer and not wanting to involve Ariane in any of his troubles, he needed to quickly lose his tail before something happened. But he needed to do it without alarming her. As they approached the upcoming traffic light she began to slow down for the yellow light. Sin waited until he seen the Malibu behind them begin to slow up before egging her on to take the light. "Take that light, let's see what this thing can do," he said looking at her.

His hypnotizing eyes pierced through her and she suddenly felt the need to obey his commands. Ariane pressed on the gas without hesitation and zoomed through the light just as it turned red. "Whoa!" she screamed as the Porsche picked up speed and raced up the street for a couple city blocks. Blind to the real reason she had been asked to open it up, she was enjoying the adrenaline rush too much to notice her passenger was distracted.

Sin looked in the rearview mirror and noticed that the Malibu was still stuck at the light. He instructed her to take the next right and after a few more turns they were back at the dealership. Upon their return Sin knew he needed to find an excuse why he wouldn't be able to take her on another test drive. He definitely wanted to spend some more time with the beautiful woman but wouldn't risk putting her in harm's way. Between him and his father's dealings it was no telling who could have been in that car. Sin always thought two to three steps ahead and was ready for whatever came his way.

"I'm sorry Ariane, I actually lost track of time. I have another appointment scheduled at any moment now and I..."

Sin spoke still attempting to sell himself as just a sales rep.

"No need to apologize. I know you squeezed me in and I appreciate all your help." She informed him.

"I would love to do this again," Sin confessed. "That is if you haven't found something else... by let's say Saturday?" he asked hoping she would say yes. "You can test drive everything on the lot until you find something you like," he promised.

"Maybe," Ariane said before taking one of his business cards.

"Call me," Sin informed her. "If you make up your mind."

"I might," she replied with a smile. She was still interested in purchasing a vehicle but the sexy salesman had definitely peaked her interest. She wasn't about to let him know it though. A return trip to the establishment was now high on her list of things to do, even if it was only for the eye candy, she thought to herself on the way out of the door.

CHAPTER 5

"Oh my God!" Ariane said finally coming to a stop after dragging the heavy box across the living room floor of her still empty apartment on the first floor of a brownstone. Her furniture was due to arrive at any moment and she needed to unpack the last few boxes that remained from her move. She had avoided it long enough. Dressed in a tight wife beater and a pink pair of track shorts, that were struggling to contain her thick round ass with every move, Ariane plopped down on the floor next to the big box and started removing the items inside. The decision to move from DC had been a hard one for her. Stepping out of her comfort zone wasn't something that she enjoyed doing, so packing up and moving to New York from the place she had lived her entire life was big for her. But the change of scenery was truly needed and welcomed.

Things back home had gotten crazy for her after the

death of her older brother Quan. He was her everything. The only father figure she had known most of her life and everything about the capital city reminded her of him. She would break down passing the park, remembering how he would let her tag along when he went to play basketball in their younger days. He used to take her almost everywhere when they were children. Not because he enjoyed her company but it was his way of keeping an eye on her, making sure she stayed out of trouble. She had taken his death hard and it finally became too much to bear so one day she woke up and started packing. At first she had no idea where she was going. First thinking of heading south to Atlanta but after remembering the fun she had on a shopping trip to New York a few years ago, she decided to give the Big Apple a shot.

Ariane was halfway through the box when she heard the doorbell ring. Hopping up from the floor, she walked over to the door and looked through the peephole. After seeing the person on the other side a wide smile came across her face as she hurried to unlock the door and swung it open.

"Heeey Girl," Faye said as her best friend's front door open.

"Hey trick," Ariane teased happy to see the familiar face before embracing her tight. "What are you doing here?" she asked pleasantly surprised.

"I rode up with K and them," she said pointing back at the moving truck parked in front of Ariane's house.

"You rode in a moving truck from DC with your brother and his crew?" Ariane questioned unable to believe her ears.

Feiben Melaku, or Faye as she was called, was very high maintenance. An Ethiopian beauty with a banging body, who had an aspiration of becoming a model but so far she had only made appearances in a few rap videos. She and Ariane had been best friends for as long as they both could remember. She didn't want to see her friend leave DC but she understood her reasons for wanting to and supported it. But it had been a few weeks since she last saw her and she missed her.

"Yes I did but only for you and never again," she confessed walking into the house.

"Where's K and them, Faye?" Ariane asked.

"They coming, they bringing your couch up the stairs," she answered heading towards the kitchen. "Who cares I need a drink. I know you got some wine in here."

Ariane just shook her head as she stood there holding the door open for the movers.

The two friends stood in the kitchen sipping wine and catching up as they watched the movers bring in the last of Ariane's furniture. The apartment finally looked like somebody lived in it. "Ok, I see you girl. This place is fly!" Faye said with a smile on her face. "A lotta room and I'm loving your kitchen. Those cabinets are everything," she continued as she refilled her glass of Moscato.

"Yea, it'll be better with my furniture in it and a couple

finishing touches," Ariane replied.

"See that's why I'm here to save the day. You have me for a whole weekend to help you make this house a home," declared Faye.

"So you came all the way here to help me make my apartment look spectacular?" Ariane replied sarcastically twisting her lips at her best friend. "You know I know better."

"Yesssss...and other things," she said on the sly.

"Yea I bet. What other things? You always got an agenda," Ariane stated with a suspicious look on her face.

"But of course!" announced Faye as she headed towards Ariane's bedroom. "Now where is your closet chick?"

"Why Faye?" Ariane asked following behind her friend.

"Cuz I need to see something," she replied.

"See what trick?"

"What sexy shit you got in here for you to wear to this party tonight, and if I may need to borrow something of yours," she said excited by the possibilities.

"Party...umm bitch do you not see the movers out there bringing shit in this crib? There are boxes from the front door to the back. I ain't going to nobody's party. And what party? How the hell you know about a party you're not even from here!" Ariane shouted.

"Bitch please, I know about anything or anybody who is somebody. We bout to hit this party up that this nigga Gavin was talking about before I left town."

"Oh my God, you still fucking with that nigga Gavin?" quizzed a surprised Ariane.

"Um yes! I never have to wait in anyone's line to get into any event. You know that nigga just got signed to them Aphilliates niggas. He run the radio in D.C right now. He's out here DJ'ing for this party tonight for some made nigga. I can't remember his name but fuck it we in that shit. Plus NY does something to me," she said rubbing her breast with her hands then sliding them down to her waist while dancing. "I don't know, it's like I be feeling extra sexy. I love the party atmosphere. So we gonna show up fashionably late of course, make our grand entrance, turn a few heads...maybe you could snatch a few valuable numbers and potentially catch you a nigga who won't mind paying some of these high as New York bills. Girl, I heard the rent out here is high than a muthafucka!" they both shared a laugh.

"News flash bitch, I'm straight! I am just fine paying my own gotdamn bills," Ariane replied confidently.

"Sure you are doll. Just tryna look out for my homegirl, that's all," Faye said.

"Of course you are," Ariane replied with a smile while shaking her head at her crazy friend.

"Fine Ms. Independent, do as you please. However, I'm only here for three days and you are going to make sure I enjoy myself. I will not sit in this house with you sorting out china and deciding on what bedroom curtains you want. We turnin' up!"

* * *

Sin stood on the outdoor terrace on the 42nd floor of the Le Parker Meriden, dressed in an all-white button up with the sleeves rolled up just below his elbows, showing off his gold Rolex, crisp jeans and Balenciaga sneakers. Also white, perfectly fitting for the All-white affair going on behind him in the Estrela Penthouse celebrating his birthday. Holding a half empty glass in his hand, he nodded his head to the music knocking from inside the party. He had made it another year, alive and free; something a lot of people in his line of work weren't able to say including his man Harv, who they had buried a few weeks ago. That fact wasn't missed by him and he planned on celebrating life to the fullest tonight with his closest comrades. Taking another sip of his drink he surveyed his surroundings and soaked in the view from high above New York City. Lost in deep thought he suddenly heard the music get louder, turning his head to look, he could see Beans coming through the door of the terrace.

"28 my nigga!" an excited Beans said. "How it feel?" he asked as he gave his friend a pound and a hug.

"I can't front it feels good," Sin said with a smile. "They said I wouldn't make it to see 21 and when I did they said I was lucky but I'd be dead before 25. So yeah, it feels real good."

"Yeah, we came a long way from two lil' niggas running

around the projects in Fort Greene." Beans said looking out at the Manhattan skyline on the warm summer night. "Started from the bottom..."

"Yeah but we got more shit to accomplish. This ain't the top my nigga."

"It's pretty damn close ma'fucka!" Beans shouted lifting his hands in the air in a celebratory fashion causing the two friends to laugh.

"But for real, I've been talking with Cassie about trying to invest in one of them casinos, either out in AC or the Foxwoods joint in Connecticut. No better way to clean up some of this bread we making," Sin said.

"Man they ain't letting no niggas get a piece of no casinos. Especially niggas like us." Beans said with his arms stretched out looking down at himself dressed in a white V-neck t-shirt, white jeans, white 1's and a bucket hat.

"Yeah maybe not." Sin laughed not wanting to press the issue. He knew in his mind it was a possibility. He had seen first-hand all the things his father had been able to do. And no matter how much he disliked his brother, he knew that if he became mayor his father's power would only grow and a lot of lucrative opportunities would come his way through Marion's influence. He would explain all of that to Beans when the time was right, but now was definitely not it. He was ready to get back inside and enjoy the party going on in his honor.

The music got louder as the doors to the terrace swung open again, but walking through them were two people who were most certainly not on the guest list; Detectives Alvarado and Harris. Closely on their heels were Sheik, Barkim and Ali.

"Yo bro, I don't know how these muthafuckas got in here," Sheik said clearly angered by their presence.

"It's cool," Sin said calmly. "Y'all go back and enjoy the party."

"You sure?" Sheik asked clearly not wanting to leave his two friends with the detectives.

Sin just nodded without replying. He was used to dealing with the two cops and knew they were there on a wild goose chase, like they were most of the time when it came to him. They didn't have anything on him but were always fishing for information about something, trying their hardest to build a case against him. Tonight's visit was most likely about the murders at the spot in the projects.

"Sin and Beans," Det. Harris said as he approached the two men.

"Dumb and Dumber," Beans retorted with a laugh.

"Oh you think that's funny?" Det. Harris asked. "Let's see how funny it is when I haul your ass down to the precinct."

"Stop wit' all the good cop bad cop shit. What's so important that you two felt the need to interrupt my birthday party?" Sin asked not in the mood for the back and forth.

"We're here about the bodies we found in the projects.

We know that was your spot that got hit and we are here to tell you that if you're thinking about handing out some street justice, don't. We are handling the investigation, so let us do our job." Det. Alvarado informed them.

"I have no idea what chu talkin' about. I own a car dealership. Maybe you could come down and buy your wife something nice," Sin said reaching in his pocket pulling out a business card. "I could get you a good deal on something brand new. How's your credit?"

"Cut the shit Sin. We know it was your spot," Det. Alvarado said.

"Like I said, I sell cars." He reiterated.

"Oh you think we are fucking playing?" Det. Harris said removing a picture of the dead bodies found in the apartment and putting it in Sin's face. "You're a drug dealer Sin. A little smarter than most but a drug dealer none the less," he said switching the pictures to a close up of Harv with his brains blown out on the floor of the apartment. "Sooner or later you all will end up like this," he said shaking the picture for emphasis.

"Ain't that your man?" Det. Alvarado asked. "Doesn't he work for you?"

"Yeah he was my friend but whatever he did for a living was his own business and none of my concern. Now if you don't mind I would like to get back to my party. You guys can leave the same way you came in." Sin said.

"We're not finished," Det. Harris said growing tired with Sin's cool act. "And we'll leave when we goddamn please."

"Nah we're finished. And you can leave now the same way you came," Sin explained before pausing. "Or there is always the alternative," he said looking over the terrace at the long drop to the street below, then back over the shoulders of the two detectives. The detectives followed his eyes turning around looking over their shoulders. To their surprise a group of large bouncers had surrounded them. Sin just smiled before continuing, "Now you gentlemen have a good night," he said as he walked around them back into the party.

"So what's it gonna be fellas?" Beans asked staring at the two men while rubbing his hands together taking great pleasure in the looks on the detective's faces.

Realizing the odds were against them, they turned and were escorted out by the group of bouncers.

Sin slid into the seat next to where Sheik and his wife, Maleekah, were chilling out enjoying the scenery. The penthouse, like the attendees, was draped out in all white, the music was banging and the bottles were popping. People posted up by the open bar, while others danced or enjoyed some of the food that was being served.

"You aight?" Sheik asked as Sin sat down. "What was that about?"

"You already know," he said. "Small thing to a giant. Look at wifey tho," Sin said getting Maleekah's attention.

"You looking good in your all white sis, got your glow on and ay'thing."

"I had to find something to fit over this big belly," she confessed rubbing her pregnant stomach. "You know I wasn't gonna miss your party bro."

Sin just smiled. He had always admired the relationship between Sheik and Maleekah. They had been with each other since high school and had a daughter together when they were both only 16. Sheik hit the streets immediately, hustling hard to provide for his girl and new daughter. In the process he caught a case and had to do 5 years up north. Maleekah held him down his whole bid, while Sin and Beans made sure her and their daughter were straight. Sheik finally got released and on his first day home he got down on one knee and popped the question with a diamond ring Sin had picked up for him the day before. Out of all the members in the crew, outside of Beans, Sin was the closest with Sheik. Once a wild youngin', considered a livewire, jail had mellowed Sheik out. He had went in a boy and matured into a well-read thoughtful man. It had made him a smarter hustler as well, realizing that every situation didn't have to end with a bullet but the understanding that some still had to and never hesitated when it was necessary to put in work.

Beans walked up on the table as the three of them were talking. "Look who I found on my way back up from downstairs," he said pointing to Cassie and Ashleigh, Sin's two sisters standing behind him.

"Hey everybody," the two women said simultaneously greeting the group of friends.

"Late like usual," Sin said standing to greet both of them with hugs. He had counted on them showing up. He knew Cassie wouldn't miss it for the world and Ashleigh never missed a chance to party.

"Fashionably," Ashleigh said embracing him tightly. "Happy Birthday!"

"You know this one here takes forever getting ready," Cassie explained while hugging him.

"Perfection takes time. Why? You don't like what you see?" Ashleigh asked while slowly and deliberately twirling around in front of Beans, giving him a long look at her nice bubble poking out in the tight fitting white dress. Ashleigh knew she was bad and had no problem letting anyone know it. Her attraction to Beans went back to her teenage days when he first started to come around with Sin. She had always been pretty but back then she was a little awkward so like her crush on him she too went unnoticed. But Ashleigh had grown into an astounding beauty; an exact replica of what her mother looked like at her age and men fawned over her where ever she went. But it still bothered her that Beans didn't react to her the way other men did. Though he did like what he seen, he never gave her the satisfaction of knowing it.

"Has anybody seen Barkim and Ali?" Sin asked.

"Last I saw them they was over by the bar," Sheik revealed. "Kyrie lil' ass runnin' round here somewhere too with his twins."

The mention of the twins made everyone except for Sin's sisters enjoy a laugh. The look of confusion on their faces was evident. After a few moments Sin decided to let them in on the joke. He explained that the twins, Cairo and Egypt, were 19-year old sisters that both considered his young protégé their boyfriend and openly shared him. What he didn't explain was that the girls were extremely loyal and deadly. They had picked up on some of the lessons that Sin and Beans had passed down to Kyrie and the young man had molded the two young ladies into female versions of himself. After a few more minutes of chatting Sin excused himself from the group. "I'll be right back."

Making his way through the crowd of party goers, hoping to locate the remaining members of his crew, he stopped in his tracks when he spotted a familiar face standing by the bar waiting on a drink. *Oh shit, what she doing here?* he thought to himself as he walked over to where the woman was standing.

"Can I have a Jack Daniels on the rocks?" Ariane asked the bartender. She had only been there a few minutes and was already ready to go home. Faye was nowhere to be found. She dipped off heading towards the DJ booth as soon as they got into the party. Ariane didn't feel right about crashing somebody's birthday to begin with but somehow she had let her friend talk her into it. Now she was standing at the bar feeling out of place while trying to blend in.

"That's a pretty strong drink ain't it?" a voice from behind her said. When she turned to see who it was she saw a familiar face. It was the handsome salesman from the car dealership she had visited earlier in the week. "Now who's stalking who?" Sin joked.

"What you doing here?" she said surprised but happy to see him again.

"I was just about to ask you the same thing," he replied.

"You want the truth?" she said for some strange reason wanting to share it with him. "My friend dragged me here with her. She is up visiting from DC and is friends with the DJ who told her about the party."

"Oh so y'all crashing," he said laughing.

"Shhh," she said putting her finger over her lips. "You gonna get me kicked out," she joked.

"Nah I'm sure y'all will be alright. The dude whose party this is, is pretty cool. He won't even trip." He informed her.

"You sure? This look like a party for one of those wannabe baller types that be feeling himself a little too hard. Get all his famous friends in one spot just so everybody can see who he know," she said bluntly.

"I can see where you coming from. Now that you mentioned it that does make a lot of sense," he said enjoying a laugh to himself as he played along. Just as a waitress came over and whispered something in his ear. "Can you excuse me for one second I have to go help with something. Please don't go anywhere I would love to finish this conversation. You gonna stay right here?" he asked.

She nodded her head, finally feeling more comfortable now that she had seen a familiar face. She watched him walk through the crowd, thinking to herself how sexy he looked with his bronze skin draped in all white. It was definitely something about him that she liked. The confident aura he carried himself with was enticing and his smile was infectious. She could tell he had a rough edge to him but he didn't flaunt it. She liked that. She continued watching him until he disappeared in the sea of people dressed in white. She was broken from her trance by a tap on the shoulder from Faye.

"Who was that fine ass nigga you was just talking to?" she asked.

"Oh that's a guy I met earlier this week at the car dealership." Ariane informed her friend.

"Oh you keepin' secrets huh chick?" she said tapping her friend.

Suddenly the music cut off and the DJ asked for everybody's attention as they brought out the cake and prepared to sing happy birthday to the man of the night. When Sin walked on stage and the crowd started to sing, Ariane's mouth dropped. The whole time she had been talking bad about the person responsible for the party she had been talking to him.

Sin watched from the stage as Ariane looked so embarrassed. He smiled and winked at her letting her know it was okay and there were no hard feelings on his part. Honestly, he felt a little bad for playing a trick on her. As he left the stage he headed right for her and her friend still standing by the bar. Carrying a slice of cake, he hoped to use as a peace offering.

Ariane clapped her hands sarcastically as he walked over to them. "Oh you got jokes," she said.

"You made it easy," he confessed. "But here I brought you the first slice of cake. No hard feelings."

"Whatever," Ariane said accepting the cake.

"Hi I'm Sin," he said turning his attention to Faye. "And you are?"

"I'm Faye, her best friend," she said looking him up and down then nodding to her friend giving her approval.

"Would y'all like to come chill with us over at the table?" he asked.

"Yeah..." Faye started to say but was quickly cut off by her friend.

"No we're gonna get going we had enough excitement for one night," she declared while hooking her arm around her friend's arm.

"Well at least let me make sure y'all get home safe. I can have the car service take you home."

"No we're fine but thanks anyway. Nice running into you again," she said as she began to walk away.

Sin couldn't let her get away that easy, not this time. It was something about her that drew him to her. Secretly he had thought about her since their meeting at the dealership. He grabbed her hand stopping her from leaving. "Hold up Ariane," he said. "I really would like to see you again but on purpose this time."

She turned looking directly into his natural bedroom eyes unable to resist having sexual thoughts about him. "I got your card remember? I'll call you."

"So it's like that?" he asked with a sheepish smile.

"Nah, I mean it, I'ma call you." Ariane insisted flashing a sexy smile before walking away leaving Sin to watch as she moved through the crowd until she disappeared.

CHAPTER 6

The caravan of vehicles snaked the winding road inside of Holy Cross Cemetery, navigating their way to what would be the final resting place for one of the most highly regarded men in organized crime's recent memory. Before his death, Carlo Brigandi, leader of New York's legendary Brigandi Family, had been the longest reigning Don out of all the "Five Families". A man of honor, he had survived an unheard of 45 year run as the boss with only one attempt being made on his life. The feat was thought to be impossible in the new era of the Mafia, which had seen disloyalty and betrayal run rampant, destroying the principles of once infallible men; the last of the true mafia chiefs, who treated men fair, helped those in need and handed down swift punishment to those foolish enough to oppose his power. Under his guidance the unification of the "Five Families" had taken place and he played a vital part in the prosperity of the group as a whole. The Commission, as it is called, flourished and had made many of men plenty of money over the years and not just the Italian wise guys. His willingness to do business with all ethnicities made him a beloved figure throughout the entire Big Apple. Evident by the large gathering of people from all walks of life that had come out to say their last goodbyes to the underworld's icon.

The funeral was worthy of an emperor. All the heads of the families had come to pay their respects, along with businessmen and a few retired politicians. Marion Holloway was amongst those in attendance; seated comfortably in the back of the luxurious Maybach next to his wife Emma, dressed in a custom tailored black Tom Ford suit with a matching scarf draped over his neck. Marion stared out the tinted windows at the multitude of headstones as his car passed them by. For years he had kept places like this in business, being responsible for his share of bodies; some by his own hands, while other's fates were sealed on his word alone. He knew death eventually came for everyone, but even being surrounded by it at the moment, he still wouldn't allow the fear of it to creep into his heart. "Thy will be done" was something he truly believed so when it was his time he was prepared to go.

His presence at the funeral was never in question. The connection between his family and Brigandi went back to before he was even born. Marion's father had run numbers for the Brigandi family in Harlem before relocating to Brooklyn and opening up a pool hall, which served as a front for the heroin operation he ran that was backed by Carlo himself. For as long as Marion could remember his family had been doing business with the Italians, something that was foreign to most black gangsters. And because of that he knew how dangerous they were as well; which was why even at a funeral he took every precaution to remain safe, including the custom made bulletproof vest he wore concealed nicely underneath his suit. And the gun he had stashed in Emma's clutch. Nate rode shot gun in the front seat aware of all the same things. As second in command he was also head of security but more than that he was Marion's best friend and would do anything to preserve his safety.

Nate Walker was originally from Shreveport, Louisiana. He had bounced around from foster home to foster home his entire childhood and had shown an inability to stay out of trouble as a teenager. His youth advisor suggested he go to the Army so he decided to enlist. He and Marion met and became fast friends while they were stationed in Korea. Every night Marion would entertain the country boy with stories about the bright lights and beautiful women of the Big Apple. Marion was discharged first but told Nate that once he was out he should make his way to New York and look him up. After returning to Louisiana for a couple of months, Nate decided to take him up on the offer. Having someone he trusts watching his back was vital to Marion at the time, as he had started to make a good amount of money in the drug game. Nate's loyalty, lack of fear, and indifference towards committing murder made him an invaluable asset to his friend's rise to power. Marion was a born leader of men and Nate was a trained killer. Together they built a mighty organization capable of taking over their territory almost unimpeded.

As the precession came to a stop in front of the burial site Nate was the first to exit the luxury vehicle, followed by Marion, and then Emma who was helped out of the car by her husband. Dressed in a black Dolce & Gabbana skirt suit with matching heels and set of tight pearls around her neck, her hair was pulled up into a simple bun but even then, she still had an understated elegance about her. Marion held her hand as they walked, leading her over to join the other mourners. In a mass of people all dressed in black, the Holloways stood out as if they wore a different hue. Nate followed closely behind as another one of Marion's soldiers stayed back by the car with a close eye on everything, including the federal agents parked in an unmarked car snapping photos of the guest as they arrived. Marion stood in a spot that had been left for him right next to Phil Catanzano as Emma sat down in front of him next to Phil's wife.

"Who ordered the dark meat?" a voice wondered aloud.

Directly across from the two men, stood Mike Di Toro, along with some of his head guys from the Martello family.

Marion just smiled as the brash mobster stared at him with distaste before whispering something into the ear of the man standing next to him. Never one to be intimidated Marion returned the menacing look just as the priest began the service.

As the service concluded and people were beginning to file out, the man who Di Toro had whispered something to approached Marion as he was talking to some of his legitimate business partners. But before the man could get to close, Nate intercepted him, impeding his path to Marion.

"What can I do for you?" Nate asked opening his suit jacket exposing the firearm he carried tucked in his waist.

"Hey, no need for all that my brother," the man said sarcastically with his hands raised to his side. "My boss would like to speak with you," he said referring to Marion.

"Then he can make an appointment like everybody else," Marion retorted.

"He's not gonna be happy you denying his request," the man said.

"And that means what to me?" Marion asked rhetorically.

Mike Di Toro watched from across the cemetery as things quickly went south fast with the guy he had sent. Never one to be showed up and needing for those in attendance to know exactly who he was and how much respect he felt he deserved, he quickly marched towards where the three men were standing with the rest of the henchmen in tow.

"Speak of the devil," Marion said, looking over the messenger's shoulder, seeing Di Toro walking right for them with his goons behind him.

"We need to talk," an aggressive Di Toro shouted causing people to turn and look.

"Like I told ya man, maybe another time," Marion said smoothly. "This ain't the place," he said referring to the agents in the car snapping pics. "But we'll have our chance," he said with a smile that hid his true intentions.

"Yeah we sure will," Di Toro said almost as a promise to run across Marion again but in a threatening manner.

Marion by that time had walked away, joining Emma as she strutted back to their waiting vehicle. She had seen everything transpire between her husband and Di Toro and wanted to make sure he was good.

"Everything alright?" she asked. "What was that about?"

Marion placed his hand on her lower back to ease her worries as he walked next to her. "Nothing you should worry about," he assured.

"Worried? I'm a Holloway my dear and we don't worry about anything," she said kissing him on the cheek, than wiping the lipstick off with her thumb before slipping into the waiting car.

CHAPTER 7

"Daddy!" five-year old Mason Jr. screamed before taking off running towards Mason, as he saw his father come through the door and sit his briefcase down. Unable to contain his enthusiasm, he wanted to tell his father all about his performance in his Little League game from earlier in the day. But after a long day on the campaign trail, a mentally drained Mason was hardly interested in anything other than dinner and a hot shower.

"Daddy let me tell you what happened today at the game..."

"Not right now MJ, where's your mother?" Mason said brushing the bright-eyed youngster off and heading for the kitchen in the luxury apartment, located on West 38th Street. The beautiful upscale home with immaculate views had recently become home for Mason, Khari and their two children, evident by the unpacked boxes still in the hallway.

Mason felt it was better for voters to see him and his family as much as possible and the apartment in the city made him seem more accessible, like one of the people. Khari would be able to smile for the cameras as she took their children to school in the morning, something Mason loved seeing in the papers. She wasn't too happy about it though, preferring the privacy of their gated community home just outside the city. But it was the beautiful views that convinced Khari to move out of her home in Westchester and into the Manhattan high rise. She had truly come a long way from her neighborhood in Brooklyn and Mason reminded her that it was him that had taken her out of it every chance he got.

"Khari!" Mason shouted as he strutted through the apartment. "I'm home, where are you?" he questioned loudly.

"In the kitchen," she yelled back.

Mason walked into the large chef style kitchen and placed his cell phone on the breakfast bar next to his wife, who was seated next to their beautiful eight-year old daughter Bria, helping her with her homework.

"Hi daddy," Bria said as she looked up from her notebook briefly to acknowledge him.

"Hey baby," Mason said as he kissed her on the top of her head. "How was school?" he asked before walking over and opening the refrigerator.

"It was good," she said focused more on her work then his attempt at small talk.

Mason turned his attention to his wife who he had ignored up until then. "What you cook for dinner?" he asked harshly seeming irritated by having to ask her anything.

"You didn't get my message? I texted your phone earlier telling you the kids wanted pizza," Khari explained. "It's in the oven."

"Pizza again?" Mason said opening the oven to peek in, then slamming it closed, startling Khari and Bria causing them to jump.

"What's your problem Mason?" Khari inquired.

"You, what the hell do you do around here all day?" he asked before exiting the kitchen.

Khari just stared off into space, unaware of what had just happened. Mason's attitude had been something she had grown use to over the years. It was something she told herself came along with being married to a politician, he's under enormous amounts of pressure and stress, was how she explained it to herself. But the luxurious lifestyle he provided her, which always seemed enough to justify his actions, was slowly losing its golden shine. After all, how many bags and shoes could he buy; how many trips could she go on, how many apologies did he have left. Khari had endured so much over the years, sacrificed her dreams as an actress to be by his side as he climbed the political ranks and now that he was on the verge of becoming mayor she felt even more obligated to see it through. The love they once shared had become a distant memory for her and she was almost positive it was for him. Their marriage had become more of a partnership than anything. She smiled when instructed and he kissed her on cue. She once was content with her lifestyle of being a trophy wife and a mother but after the years carried on, Khari realized she had no life outside of Mason and her children, not to mention her mother in law Emma, who seemed to have a constant opinion on everything including their marriage. At times she wasn't sure if she'd said I do to Mason or Emma.

Khari pulled the pizza out the oven and sat it on top of the counter next to Bria. "Baby give me a second and I'll make you and your brother's plate. Daddy is tired. I'm gonna go in the room and see if he is ready to eat something," she said to her daughter, who kept her head in her books. She was used to her parents' interaction, so her father verbally disrespecting her mother was now a norm. Khari walked down the double wide foyer of the apartment towards the double doors that led into their master suite. When she walked in, Mason was unbuttoning his shirt and headed into the bathroom for a shower.

"Why do you show your ass in front of the kids all the time?" she spoke out loud while shutting the bedroom doors.

"Please, don't you think they should have a decent meal on a Monday?" Mason replied sarcastically.

"Well I let them vote on dinner tonight because after I picked up MJ from his game it was already late. I knew Bria had to study for her test tomorrow, so we decided on something quick, but what is the fuckin' problem Mason? It's like you have to find something to complain about, nothing I do is ever good enough for you anymore. I wear my hair a certain way you got something to say. I wear a tad bit of extra foundation on my face and you notice it enough to complain about it, instead of complimenting me. Am I your wife or a fucking punching bag?!" she screamed.

Not moved by Khari's words, Mason stepped into their jetted shower and chuckled to himself.

"What the fuck do you want Khari, a medal of honor?" he questioned while clapping his hands together as a sarcastic gesture. "I bust my ass out here kissing hundreds of white muthafucka's asses to get their votes, and for who? Not just for me princess, I do it so that you can continue wearing all that fancy shit like you're fucking Michelle Obama or somebody. I put on the show and you just have to wave your hand and support me. That's all. So if I feel like complaining about not wanting pizza when I get home I shouldn't get no lip about it," Mason proclaimed.

Kari just stared at the fogged image of her husband in the shower and shook her head, amused by her husband's statements. "You just don't get it do you?" was all she said before she exited the bathroom and headed towards the door.

"Get what? That you're a fucking spoiled cry baby, c'mon give me a break!" Mason spat continuing to hurl insults, but by that time Khari was out of the room and out of ear shot.

CHAPTER 8

Ashleigh Holloway sashayed into Club Mirage looking like a star. All the hustlers and wannabe hustlers were out tonight and every eye in the spot seemed to be trained on her. Ashleigh was Marion and Emma's youngest daughter and a spitting image of her mother. Her whole lifestyle had been afforded by her parents and at the age of twenty-five, it didn't bother her one bit that she hadn't done anything productive with her life. Shopping and traveling was what she specialized in. When it came to Ashleigh, spoiled was an understatement. Although she obtained her real estate license four years ago, she had yet to put it to use. She had no plans to either; she had only gotten it to keep her father from complaining. She enjoyed being the princess of the family and wore her tiara with pride and selfishness. She fashioned herself a socialite, partying all over the city almost every night of the week. Tonight, she stepped out with her two home girls Trina and

Michelle. They were more like her pet projects than her friends. She made sure they stayed below her level; enough to be good enough to hang with, but not prettier than her or flyer than her. Her mother always taught her to never keep bitches in her circle who had expectations to become better than her, and never keep bitches around her who weren't worthy of her presence. Whatever that was supposed to mean. But it seemed to make sense to her.

Ashleigh and her crew took their seats at the V.I.P table closest to the DJ booth, within seconds the waitress came over to take their drink orders. Ashleigh ordered two bottles of Ciroc, one coconut, one red berry and a bottle of Ace of Spade. She didn't intend on her and her crew finishing any of the bottles but to her it was all about the look. The waitress immediately went to put the girls order through and Ashleigh and her girls sat vibing to the sounds of the new Rico Love song.

"Do you see the crowd? There's crazy bread in here tonight!" said an excited Trina.

"Girl bye! Niggas bread ain't long enough for me in here. If you ain't the nigga depositing the bank statements in this place at the end of the week with your name on it, you ain't possibly got no rap for a bitch like me!" replied Ashleigh.

"I'm saying, that nigga Case is in here tonight and that nigga got hella bread! And that nigga is respected. Ma'fuckas know not to front on that nigga or his people and you know

I got a thing for a nigga with authority!" Michelle said before slapping five with Trina.

"Y'all bitches got a lot to learn," Ashleigh said and chuckled. "If a nigga had authority like y'all say, it wouldn't be so easy for y'all to notice. That nigga is loud and I mean that in the way he moves. Real G's move in silence and so does real money." Ashleigh said schooling her protégés. Although the whole time she never took her eyes off of Case, who was sitting in the other V.I.P section with his crew. She couldn't help but secretly admire how sexy he was, everything about his look was right. She would never approach him, but she might consider entertaining his conversation if he made his way to her. The whole time Beans had been watching Ashleigh and her crew through the one way mirror in his office above the bar.

Beans was the owner of Mirage, he and Sin had been in the game together since young niggas and the club was one of the investments he made from years of hustling. They both tried to legitimize their earnings by cleaning it up in businesses; Sin with the dealership and Beans with the club. He knew for a fact that Sin would disapprove of his baby sister being in the club that night or any night for that matter, as he knew the type of crowd that frequented Beans' spot. Mostly low level hustlers, stick up kids and bitches looking to come up, but it was still the hottest spot in Brooklyn and on any given night somebody who was somebody would show up.

Beans had always admired Ashleigh's beauty and her stuck up attitude didn't seem to bother him at all. Her spoiled ways usually ran most men away but it actually turned him on. She was a rebellious hot head, sort of like him. She did everything she knew her family would disapprove of, especially Sin, who she would constantly bump heads with over her propensity for being in the wrong places around unsavory characters. She could be anywhere she wanted to be on any given night but she loved being in the hood, chasing a lifestyle she never lived. She knew all the right things to say to fit in but to any real street nigga she stuck out like a sore thumb. It was always about a look for Ashleigh; always a bad bitch contest and she knew most females wherever she went, were runner ups on her worst day. Beans never blatantly showed his interest in Ashleigh purely out of respect for his boy. Sin had never indicated if he would approve or not, but Beans saw it as a complication he didn't need. He instead showed it in other ways; he would make sure she made it home safely after a long night of partying in the city and he would personally keep an eye on her anytime he spotted her somewhere she wasn't supposed to be.

Beans made his way down the spiral staircase from the club's office towards Ashleigh's table. She noticed him making his way to her but tried to act as if she didn't, turning towards her friends and swinging her shoulder back and forth to the music. "Here this hating ass nigga come," she mumbled to herself.

Beans sat across from the three women as if he was invited. Ashleigh said nothing but both Michelle and Trina welcomed him with a smile and a "Heeey Beans," unable to deny how sexy and gutter he looked in his black Gucci polo shirt and Brooklyn Nets snapback cocked to the side. Beans wasn't the prettiest nigga but he was what a bitch would call right. He was 5 foot 11 with a light caramel complexion and a solid built, one hundred seventy-five pound frame that was covered in tattoos. He sported a tapered fade with 360 waves and he wore a scar on the left side of his cheek, but it took nothing away from his sex appeal; the scar actually enhanced it. Beans was about his business and niggas wanted no problems with him and he liked it that way. Grabbing one of the glasses off the table he poured himself some of the red berry Ciroc without responding to the two women's greeting. He instead directed his attention towards Ashleigh, before taking a drink from his glass he tilted it towards her signaling he was toasting to her. "Y'all ladies enjoyin' yaselves tonight?" Beans asked staring directly at Ashleigh.

She never replied but Trina jumped at the opportunity to chat with him. "Yea, we cool!"

"It's poppin' in here tonight," Michelle said.

Ashleigh gave them a look like as if to ask why they were entertaining him. She knew his question was pure sarcasm and she twisted up her lips and looked away letting him know she wasn't interested in his small talk.

"Wassup over there Ash, you good?" Beans inquired.

"I'm great Beans. How you feeling?" Ashleigh replied sarcastically.

"I would be doing a lot better if you and your cronies were to get the fuck up outta here. You know you don't belong in here and I would hate for Sin to come in here and see you. You know he don't like you hanging out at these type of spots, it's too much of a risk," Beans replied.

"And what are you, Sin's watchdog? No, let me guess you are here to babysit me huh? Look nigga, if I needed a babysitter I would hire one! I'm all the way good." Ashleigh boldly responded.

Beans just laughed at the feisty beauty. "I hear all that ma, but check this out, I'ma leave you ladies to do whatever the fuck it is that y'all do and I'll be in my office." He said before taking a big gulp finishing off his drink. "If you need me, you know where to find me. And when I'm ready for you to leave, you will leave, no questions asked," he continued, making it clear to Ashleigh that despite all her tough talk he still controlled shit. "In the meantime enjoy yourselves," he said smiling as he got up from the table and walked back towards his office.

"That nigga be blowing mine," Ashleigh said as she sipped her champagne.

"Shit, that nigga could blow mine any day! And I might

consider blowing him if he made it worth my time!" Trina said causing Michelle to laugh, almost spitting out her drink.

Ashleigh smirked at her girlfriends while they shared a laugh but felt slightly aggravated knowing Beans was all on her like a cheap suit. "I'm going to the ladies room, y'all bitches are stupid," she said standing up adjusting her dress pulling it down past her thighs. She walked to the bar towards the sign that read restrooms on her way, passing Case's table where he was partying with his crew.

Case spotted Ashleigh and immediately directed his attention towards her, leaving his man Dre in a conversation by himself. He had been watching her all night and knew that before he dipped out, he was gonna holla at her. He didn't know what type of female she was so he didn't know if she would be something he could skate out with before the night was over, but he knew he had intentions on linking with her in the near future. What Case wanted he usually got, so he tried to do a little homework before he approached her.

"Yo, who shorty in the white? You know that chick?" Case asked Dre, cutting him off in his one sided conversation.

"Nah, I ain't never seen shorty before. Why wassup?" asked Dre.

"I need to find out," he said stepping from around his table. "Hold me down," Case said as he made his way towards the bathrooms with Dre trailing a few steps behind.

He turned the corner just in time to see Ashleigh being

harassed by a young hustler that seemed to be unwilling to let her hand go as he tried to spit his game. Not only did she appear to be uninterested, she had a look of frustration on her face as he was impeding her path to the bathroom. Frustration turned to anger as she was barely able to hold her pee any longer.

"Would you let go of my hand," she shouted as she jerked to pull away. "I said I'm good the first time."

"Bitch who the fuck you think you talking to," the unruly hustler spoke with discourtesy. "You should be lucky a nigga like me trying to holla at you."

"Bitch?" she repeated. "Nigga, you better get the fuck outta my face before you be on somebody's t-shirt," she raged.

Case, impressed by her fiery spirit, decided to help her out of her current situation. "Hey ma, what's taking you so long?" he shouted as he strolled down the hallway towards them causing them both to look back at him. "Yo, my man what the fuck are you doin'? Get ya hands off my girl," he instructed.

Seeing Case walking towards him, the young hustler quickly released his grip on Ashleigh. He was certainly aware of who Case was and definitely didn't want that issue. He immediately began to cop pleas the closer Case got. "My bad Case, I didn't know that she was your lady. I meant no disrespect."

"You know me my nigga?" Case asked.

"Nah but I know of you."

"But do you know me?" Case repeated.

"Nah."

"Then don't call me by my name like we cool."

"Like I said I meant no disrespect," the young hustler said now seeing Dre standing behind Case clearly strapped.

"Go head ma and go to the bathroom. I'll be right here when you get out," he said looking at Ashleigh. "This nigga won't though," he barked staring at the apologetic hustler, causing him to put his head down before walking away.

Ashleigh checked herself out in the mirror. She needed to look perfect before she would even consider exiting the bathroom. While she applied some lip gloss, she couldn't help but think about how Case had come to her defense and though she knew he wasn't at the level of niggas she was used to fucking with, a small part of her hoped he would still be by the door when she came out.

Case watched as the door to the women's bathroom swung open and Ashleigh came strutting out. He leaned off the wall, prepared to engage in a conversation but she calmly walked past him as if he was invisible.

"Hold up ma," he said trying to get her attention. "Can I speak with you for a second?" he asked.

Ashleigh stopped in her tracks and spun around looking him up and down. "What were you waiting for, a thank you?" she said arrogantly.

"No not at all," he said.

"Oh, because I didn't need or ask for your help," she insisted.

"I could see that you handled yourself very well," he complimented. "Let me walk you back to your table though. These nobody ass niggas in here be on some bullshit, but ain't nobody gonna try nothing if you with me," he informed her.

"Is that right?" she asked liking his confidence. "So you're a somebody?"

"Yea, I'm Case ma," he said with a smile. He was strikingly handsome and he knew it.

"I've never heard of you," Ashleigh proclaimed.

"You have now," he said. "But check this out I'm about dip out in a few. You care to join me?"

Ashleigh just laughed. *What does he take me for?* she thought to herself. *Some jump off that would just slide with him because he pressed some nigga in the club for me, please.* She could tell that he was used to getting his way with women, his looks and his hood status got him his fair share of pussy. But she was also used to having her way with men and wasn't going to give in that easy. "Excuse me?" she retorted.

"My bad that came out wrong. I was seeing if you wanted to go get sumtin' to eat?" he quickly corrected himself. "I know a soul food spot that stay open all night."

"No I'll pass," she said. "But maybe another time."

"You sure?" he asked but she just nodded confirming her

answer. "Cool, well let me get your number in case I get into something. I might need some back up after seeing how you handled ya self and shit." He joked finally getting a smile out of her.

The two exchanged numbers and walked separately back to their tables. Ashleigh never said a word to her girls about her encounter with Case. She just enjoyed the rest of her night but every now and then she would look over at his table and catch him watching her. His seductive stares made her wet. Ashleigh knew sometime soon she was going to fuck him, she just hoped he fucked as good as he looked. Case and his crew eventually got up and exited the club leaving her with only her lustful thoughts of him.

CHAPTER 9

Sin picked up his office phone on the second ring, held it to his ear with his shoulder and continued counting the money stacked on his desk. The large amount of cash had just been delivered inside the roof of one of the cars in a shipment he had received, another successful transaction. The organization had begun to see a substantial increase in profits and the money was coming in fast. Sin was dropping off cash to Cassie at twice the rate he had been before and while she was still able to invest it, clean it and stash it, the influx of money had become increasingly harder to manipulate. Marion had a plan though and he had called a family meeting a few days from now to discuss it.

"Hello, Manhattan Motorcars." Sin spoke into the phone.

"Hello, may I speak with Yasin please?" the angelic voice on the other end spoke and rang familiar to him.

"Speaking," he said.

"Hey Sin, this is Ariane." Was all he needed to hear for him to start smiling.

"How you doing?" Sin asked. "So you kept your word. I like that."

"I always do," she informed him. "What about you?"

"What about me?" he asked.

"Are you a man of your word?" Ariane asked.

"Of course."

"Well you told me whenever I was ready to look at some more cars to give you a call, so I was wondering if I could come in today and test drive a few." She inquired putting on her most innocent sounding voice.

Sin had been intrigued by the gorgeous woman and really wanted to see her again but having her come into the dealership wasn't really what he had in mind. Thinking quickly he came up with an idea. "I was about to step out of the office for a few but I have an idea if you are up to it?" he informed her. "I have a car in mind that I think you would really like. I have some quick errands to run but I can take the car out with me and be to you within the next hour when I'm finished. This way you can test drive the vehicle for as long as you like."

Ariane had been thinking about Sin ever since she had left the party and she was not about to turn down the opportunity to spend some extended time with him. "Well we can do it another time if it is an inconvenience to you," she said giving him a hard time but really joking.

"C'mon it's not a problem at all," he said reassuring her. "Let me get a pen to take down the address."

* * *

Ariane hung up the phone and immediately raced towards her closet. She had less than an hour to get ready and be at the address she gave Sin over the phone. Not being blinded by his good looks and charm, she gave him an address of a coffee shop a few blocks away, not wanting to reveal her address in case he turned out to be the crazy stalker type. She needed something sexy without looking like she was trying too hard. Being overdressed would be a dead giveaway that she was really interested in him and not knowing his true intentions, she wasn't about to look foolish. Before she could decide on what she wanted to wear, she ransacked her closet. Her room looked like a tornado hit it with all the thrown together ensembles she tried to put together. She finally decided to go with her favorite pair of high waist jeans that made her ass look perfect, a white top and a pair of black Ferragamo pumps. She showered and indulged her body in her Victoria Secret Simply Breathless body lotion because the scent was soft but made its statement. After she dressed she pulled her hair back into a tight ponytail letting her soft curls hang freely from the scrunchie holding her hair together. She applied some eyeliner and her favorite MAC lip gloss to her face. To finish off her masterpiece she grabbed her all black Roberto Cavalli shades and placed them on her face. She stared in the mirror for a few seconds second guessing and admiring her outfit at the same time. Ariane wanted to impress Sin without showing him that was what she was trying. She thought everything about him was sexy; from the way he dressed to the way he talked and stared at her after asking her a question. For some reason he made her stomach feel funny when she was around him; not a sickening feeling to it, but a nervous feeling, one she actually liked. After leaving Sin that night at the party, the thought of him ran through her mind constantly. She would catch that feeling whenever he crossed her thoughts, and when she was alone imagining his face made her pussy purr. Snapping herself out of her thoughts, she glanced at her rose gold Michael Kors watch and saw she had fifteen minutes to be at the spot where she was meeting him. *Shit I can be fashionably late*, she thought, but the anticipation was killing her. Ariane grabbed her bag and keys then headed out the door.

I hope he is on time, she thought as she got into the waiting taxi.

Ariane pulled up to the coffee shop five minutes early.

She paid the cab driver, got out and walked into the Starbucks on the corner, taking a seat at the last table by the window so that she could see Sin when he pulled up. *He's got 10 minutes to be here. If not I am leaving,* Ariane thought to herself. Her nervousness made her feel that way but she knew she wasn't going to go anywhere. She planned on waiting there in hopes of not being stood up. Ariane pulled out her iPhone and scrolled through her messages and social media notifications to kill time while she waited. She ordered a cappuccino but it just sat in front of her. She was too nervous to drink anything but didn't want to sit in the coffee shop without ordering. It had been over a year since she was last on a date and longer than that she had been in a relationship. Plenty of guys tried getting at her but she just never seemed to be interested in any of them. Ariane continued scrolling through her phone as she waited. When her text message notification came across her screen, she opened it and it read: *Hey beautiful are you just gonna sit there with your nose in your phone? Or you wanna ride out?* Ariane's heart palpated a few times when she realized Sin was outside and had been watching her. She smiled before looking up and out the window and spotted him. He was parked and sitting on the passenger side of a white Range Rover looking directly at her. Ariane left a five-dollar bill on the table and made her way towards the door of the shop, still nervous but very happy to see him again.

"Hello," Ariane said as she slid into the driver's seat, with a huge smile on her face. "Nice seeing you again."

"Likewise," Sin answered admiring her. "You smell good."

"Thank you."

"But you look better," he said causing her to smile.

"Flattery will get you everywhere," she joked.

"And I came bearing gifts," he pointed the Range Rover.

"Now this is all the way me," Ariane said as she cruised New York City's traffic. Although the roads were not smoothly paved the white Range Rover Sin chose for her glided through the streets easily.

"Oh you like this, huh? I figured you would. Ya'll look good together," said Sin flirtatiously.

Ariane smiled at his comment and kept looking straight ahead. He had the truck smelling so good with the scent of his *Unforgivable* cologne, and was looking even better. The feeling she got being around him was one she hadn't felt in what seemed like forever, and she loved it when he talked to her. He alerted places in her body that had been dormant for a long time.

"Do you mind turning down that block, then making a right?" Sin asked.

"No problem," replied Ariane

"I just need to make a quick stop. You not in a rush or anything are you?"

"Uh no, it's cool this was kind of my afternoon plans,"

she assured him.

A big smile came across his face before he said, "Good, cause you mine all day."

"Oh am I?" Ariane replied surprisingly but happy at the same time.

"Listen I ain't gonna front cuz that ain't me. I've been thinking about you ever since the first day at the dealership. When I saw you at my party I was buggin', cause I had been thinking about what I was gonna to do to see you again and then there you were."

Ariane took in his words like music to her ears she couldn't help but smile, admire and respect the honesty that was coming out of his mouth. If this was game at this time she was open to it because without saying she wanted the same exact thing that he wanted.

"Pull up right here and park," Sin instructed her.

She parked in front of Peter Lugers in the Williamsburg section of Brooklyn. Sin got out of the passenger side and came around to open her door. "I hope you hungry. I took the liberty to make us reservations for lunch," he said grabbing her by her hand and helping her down from the truck.

"You really had this planned out didn't you?" an impressed Ariane gushed.

"Yea I did, I'm kind of what you call a risk taker. I figured you could either say I ate already or I don't want to eat here. And in that case I would have taken you anywhere you wanted to go in the city." They both shared a laugh.

Ariane was definitely impressed by his charming demeanor and his take charge approach and she couldn't wait to learn more about him as well. They walked in the restaurant and the hostess greeted Sin by his last name.

"Mr. Kennedy right this way sir," the short middle aged woman directed them to a booth secluded off in a part of the restaurant that had not even been open for business yet; she had to remove the red velvet rope to let them pass. Ariane took notice of all the special treatment Sin was receiving. She knew he had to be a little more than just a car salesman, but she didn't say a word, just quietly prayed to herself that whatever it was that he did wasn't illegal. They sat at a booth that had a perfect view of the Williamsburg Bridge. The scene was beautiful and by now her jaws were aching because she couldn't seem to get rid of the smile on her face.

"Tell me about yourself," Sin asked as he leaned back into his seat.

"What would you like to know?" she replied showing a little nervousness. She could tell he was different from any other nigga she dealt with. He held a charisma that she was unfamiliar with, and in his dark brown eyes she could tell that he had seen or encountered a lot in his young years. He was street without being hood, a quality she found so appealing.

"Everything," he replied. "You can start from the beginning if you like, as far back as you can remember. I want to know everything about you. What elementary school you went to? Who was the first boy you kissed? Did you used to pee in the bed?" he said with a smile.

"Really?" she said busting out laughing.

"Really," he said still joking and flashing a smile. "But seriously, I'm intrigued by you and there are not many people who do that for me, so help me get to know you. Let's start with something simple, where you from?"

"I'm from DC...Uptown, Georgia Ave. to be exact. What about you?"

"I'm from Brooklyn, born and raised in Fort Greene," he said proudly. "How long you been living here?" he asked.

"Not long, a month." She confessed.

"Really?" he said laughing. "Damn, what made you move to New York? If you don't mind me asking."

Her eyes immediately looked down at the table and the smile that was once on her face disappeared. Sin could see that it was a touchy subject; one that she didn't feel comfortable enough sharing at the moment and he respected her privacy. Although he truly wanted to know what caused the look of hurt and pain that had quickly consumed her face, he didn't want to press her. His only hope was that one day she would feel comfortable enough to trust him with her heart and divulge her innermost secrets to him. He wanted to be the one to help her mend whatever it was that pained her.

"So what is it that you do for a living?" he asked quickly

changing the subject.

"I'm in the restaurant business," she said.

"Oh so you own a restaurant?" he questioned.

"No, I'm a chef. Well I was back home. I came here with hopes of owning my own restaurant someday soon. I have some money saved so we will see."

"So you can cook?" Sin said smiling. "But let me ask you this, if you're looking into buying your own restaurant, why you wanna waste money on buying a fancy car?" he wondered aloud.

Ariane just laughed. "Ok I got a confession," she said as she continued to giggle. "I can't afford none of the cars you sell," she said staring in his now confused face. "I have goals in life and I'm a person who is motivated by the things I want. So test driving an expensive car or taking a tour of a house I can't afford at the moment gives me the drive to go get those things. It may sound silly to you but it works for me. It always has."

"Nah it doesn't sound silly at all." He truly understood her drive. He had seen it in by the look in her eyes. It was the same one he had when he was determined to not to spend his life on the block as a hand to mouth hustler.

"Now let me ask you a question and answer this honestly. What is it that you do for a living?" she inquired.

"I sell cars," he said.

"I never seen or met a car salesman like you and the type

of birthday parties you throw. The way people react to you. The special treatment you receive, like us sitting in a private area in this restaurant. Who can take cars from their jobs and go out on dates with them?" she asked.

Sin laughed, it was now his turn to confess. "Ok I got my own confession."

Ariane held her breath waiting for him to tell her what he really did. *I knew it, he's too good to be true,* she thought to herself. *I was just starting to like you.*

"I don't sell cars at all. I actually own the dealership," he revealed. "I saw you on the showroom floor and pretended to be a salesman.

Ariane was relieved. She actually thought it was flattering that he had gone out his way to meet her.

The two sat having lunch and talking for hours. When they were finished Sin took her on a tour of New York City. After hours of sightseeing they ended up at the Promenade back in Brooklyn staring at Manhattan.

"Thank you for the tour, I really enjoyed myself." Ariane expressed.

"Me too." Sin said.

"I don't know why I feel so comfortable with you," she confessed.

"You don't have a reason not to," he informed her as he pulled her into his embrace and she laid her head on his chest. "I don't have any intentions of hurting you."

"Nobody ever does. But they do," she said.

"New city, new beginnings," he told her hoping to ease whatever it was that she was holding on to from her past. "You can't be scared forever."

"Ain't nobody scared," she said hitting him in his chest.

"Give me a kiss then," he smoothly said as he looked her in her eyes.

Once again those bedroom eyes made him irresistible, almost hypnotizing as she leaned in to kiss him. His lips were soft and she instantly knew she had made the right choice. Before she knew it, she had slipped her tongue into his mouth. Their tongues met and danced inside of each other mouths, perfectly in step with one another. Ariane could feel herself beginning to get moist and her pussy starting to purr. Sin's hands slid down her back and he used both hands to palm her nice thick ass. She could feel his manhood becoming rock hard in his jeans as she rubbed up against him. That only seemed to turn her on more. Trying to regain her composure and take control of the situation before they were both out of their clothes having sex in public, she pulled back from him but not before getting one last lick of his juicy lips.

"It's getting late. I think I'm ready to go home," she said in between deep breaths.

Sin stood there with his man at full attention in his jeans, so hard it becoming was uncomfortable. Never one to press the issue, he snapped back into reality realizing that they were in public. "Yeah, you're right, it is late." He said checking his watch.

The two of them rode in the truck on the way to her house not saying much to one another. It was almost like they were still coming down off of a high and didn't want to mess it up for the other one. The only words spoken had been Ariane giving him directions to her house. Sin pulled up to the curb and parked in front of her brownstone and cut off the engine.

"I really enjoyed spending the day wit' you..." he said just as she leaned over and kissed him, opening her mouth, allowing his tongue to slip in once again. They continued passionately kissing while she took her hand and began rubbing his dick through his jeans making it swell once again. Ariane reached back opening the car door and seductively slid out of her seat.

Now standing on the sidewalk with the door open, she looked at Sin in the driver's seat and said, "C'mon, you not getting away that easy." Then she turned and walked up the steps towards her door.

CHAPTER 10

Ariane entered her dimly lit apartment and dropped her keys, bag and shoes at the door. The adrenaline pumping through her body had her heart pounding in her chest. She hadn't felt this much nervous energy in a while. She knew that the smallest bit of trepidation that she allowed to creep into her mind would definitely cause her to abort her mission. It had been so long since she felt a man's touch and right now she wanted to feel this man inside of her. Ariane never looked back or gave any directions; she just headed for her bedroom, which was directly down the hallway from her front door. Every step she took, one of her garments dropped to the floor. Sin stood with his back against the apartment door, admiring Ariane's sexy body as she slowly revealed it to him. His erection growing larger with every piece of clothing that hit the floor.   Finally, she reached the room, laying invitingly across the bed and locking her eyes on the man headed down the hallway towards her. Sin pulled his shirt over his head as he strutted into the bedroom wearing a white wife beater. His bronze skin looked so smooth and the sharpness of his sleeve tattoo added to his sexiness. Sin removed the wife beater, revealing the rest of his athletically built body that was covered in more tattoos. Ariane's juice box moistened at the sight of his six pack with the V as she rubbed her hand over her right breast, feeling the hardness of her nipple. Sin stood at the foot of the bed staring at her like a sex goddess. After a few seconds he unlatched his belt, unzipped his pants and let them fall to the ground, revealing his rock hard imprint in his black boxer briefs. Ariane let out a deep breath and soft moan when her eyes met it. Sin grabbed her legs, pulling her to the edge of the bed as Ariane laid her head back deciding to let him have his way with her. Fuck it, if he thinks I'm a hoe after this, I don't care. I'm gonna enjoy every inch of this man tonight, she thought to herself. For a while she had been the chief in command of her body, so it felt good to let someone take over the reins. Sin did exactly that. He kneeled down at the foot of her bed and began kissing her inner thigh softly. His full lips felt wonderful on her skin causing her to quiver. Oh yes, she thought, his touch and kiss was oh so right.

Sin explored her body, placing his face on her black cotton panties inhaling her scent. "You smell so good," he whispered reaching his right hand above his head and rubbing her breasts. Ariane closed her eyes, enjoying his touch as he slid her panties down past her ankles and tossed them on the dresser before diving tongue first into her clean shaven pussy. He licked her in circular motions until her moans grew louder, than began sucking her clit until it stiffened and welcomed it with ease into his mouth. Ariane worked her pussy on his face, unable to control herself as he drank from her love fountain, pleasing her as though he was familiar with her body. When he felt her body tense for a climax, he gripped her hips so that she couldn't pull away. She tried to push his head away to control the cries of her orgasm but he sucked on her until she was finished. As soon as her body relaxed Sin flipped her over, aggressively spreading her ass cheeks, licking her from back to front not missing a spot. Ariane was in heaven as she laid on her stomach as Sin came up and gently laid on her back brushing her hair behind her ear with his index finger and whispering, "You good?"

"Oh yes!" she moaned out as he inserted his thickness in her wet pussy. Sin let out a low moan as they connected and began giving her long strokes while she laid on her stomach, gripping the sheets until she arched her back, tooting her ass up in the air. Sin grabbed both her arms pulling them behind her and began to fuck her harder as she came on his dick. Ariane pushed away from him as he laid down on his back with his dick at attention waiting for her to take over. His body was beautiful to her and she showed her appreciation as she placed soft kisses on his chest. Her beauty had him mesmerized. He hadn't felt a connection with a woman like this in what seemed like forever. He was able to have any choice of women he wanted, but he knew she was different. Her look, her touch, her smell, at that moment he just wanted to make love to her like she had been his woman for years. Ariane climbed on top of him and used her right hand to place his glazed dick inside her again. She began to ride him with slow strides, letting the head of his dick grind on her G-spot as she moaned in pure ecstasy.

I'm not ready to cum. I'ma enjoy this pussy, he thought, biting his lip as he enjoyed her pussy walls gripping his throbbing manhood. Sin palmed her plump ass cheeks and made her motion faster and faster until Ariane came again. Feeling her cum dripping down his dick, Sin flipped her over so they were now face to face. They locked tongues passionately as he powerfully thrust in and out of her as she dug her manicured nails in his chiseled back until he felt himself reaching his peak. Sin screamed as he pulled out and came on her stomach before collapsing on the bed next to her. I'm gonna love loving her, he thought, as he stared at her laying there with her eyes closed, unaware that she was thinking the exact same thing.

CHAPTER 11

Sin rolled over reaching out hoping to get a grasp of the sexy woman he fell asleep next to but to his surprise he felt nothing but cool sheets. Slowly opening his eyes, he realized he was in the bed alone. Sitting up, allowing his eyes to adjust to the sun that was creeping through the curtains in the room, he scanned his surroundings looking for any traces of Ariane. After seeing none, he rolled out of bed and slipped on his jeans that were still lying at the foot of the bed. Exiting the bedroom, he could hear the sound of water running and pots clinging. Entering the kitchen, he saw Ariane standing over the sink.

Dressed only in his wife beater, which looked like a dress on her, she had her long hair pulled back into a pony tail. Her firm breasts sat up perky and he could see the imprint of her hard nipples on the front of the shirt. Looking up, seeing him standing there, Ariane smiled. "Good morning sleepy head," she playfully said.

"I usually don't sleep this late. Shit I don't get much sleep to begin with," he admitted.

"It's ok, you must feel comfortable in my bed," she said as her smile widened.

"Yo something smells good," he said taking in a big whiff.

"You hungry...have a seat," she ordered.

Ariane sashayed over to the breakfast bar with a plate in her hand, placing it down in front of him. She woke up early, putting her chef skills to work crafting a delicious brunch hoping to impress him. She cooked for a living but was still on edge as he prepared to taste her food for the first time. She felt butterflies around him, a nervous energy like a school girl around her childhood crush. The unspoken confidence he carried himself with was so attractive to her, the silent strength she saw when she looked in his eyes made her feel comfortable and safe in his presence. She wanted him, and after the way he sent her body into orbit the night before those feelings had only grown stronger.

"Damn, this look good," he proclaimed laying eyes on the food on the plate in front of him.

"Just a lil' catfish, shrimp and grits, N'awlins style," she bragged.

"Oh yeah," he said grabbing his fork and getting a taste. He quickly began nodding his head in approval as he continued chewing. "Your chef skills are on point," he acknowledged after swallowing.

Ariane just smiled as she sat her plate down and took the seat next to him. On the inside she was doing cartwheels, delighted by his approval. Calm down Ariane, before this man think he got you like that, she thought to herself. She had always maintained control when it came to dealing with niggas and relationships. Her brother had schooled her to the game almost from day one. Rarely did she let her feelings get involved, she witnessed first-hand some of his exploits and how he had played his share of females. He would always remind her, "*Niggas out here is foul by nature. The game ain't nothing but a pussy race. That nigga talking sweet, bringing you flowers and shit, he be the foulest one. And good girls get it the worst cuz y'all ain't nothing but a fuck trophy to a nigga.*" Quan always kept it tall with her and for the most part she had lived by those lessons, but something about Sin made her question all her rules. Sleeping with him the way she had was definitely out of her character. As she sat there enjoying her food, she began to feel the need to make that clear to him. "Sin I don't want you to think—"

"I don't, so you ain't even gotta go there," he said cutting her off before sipping his juice. "I don't know what you used to but that ain't me."

Before she was able to reply, his phone could be heard going off in the bedroom. Sin stood up from the table and headed into the back to retrieve his phone. Ariane collected their dishes and took them over to the sink and began washing them. After a few minutes Sin re-emerged from the bedroom fully dressed to her surprise. "Where you going?" she questioned, caught off guard.

"I gotta bounce. I need to go take care of something." Sin said.

"Oh ok," she said doing her best not to show her disappointment.

"Here," he said removing the key to the Range Rover from his pocket and placing it in her hand.

"What is this? I can't take this," Ariane objected.

"Why not?" he asked.

"Cuz I can't be bought," she said extending her arm to return the key.

"Bought?" Sin said shaking his head. "What I just tell you? That ain't me. That right there is a loan," he explained pointing at the keys in her hands. "Something to drive until you're able to afford one of those cars of your dreams," he said flashing that irresistible smile.

"Well, do you need a ride somewhere?" she asked giving in to him.

"Nah I'm good. I'll call you later," he said before kissing her and disappearing out the front door.

CHAPTER 12

The two guards circled the car placing the inspection mirrors under the vehicle checking for any tracking devices or bombs. Satisfied with what they saw, they motioned for the car to proceed. Beans pulled through the gates of the immaculate Holloway Estate located in Scarsdale in Westchester County, with Sin in the passenger seat. The home had always remained tightly guarded with Marion sparing no expense to ensure his family's safety. Upon their entrance both men took notice of the increased amount of armed men strategically positioned throughout the compound. Exiting the vehicle just in front of the door, they were stopped from entering by an oversized guard standing in their way demanding to pat them down. Uncle Nate opened the front door and instructed for the guard to let them pass. Sin shot the guard a menacing look as he passed him on his way into the house. Uncle Nate, seeing the look on his face, quickly informed him that the guard was new and meant no harm; he simply was just doing his job. But he could see that the explanation hadn't done much to change the look on his nephew's face.

Nate led the two of them through the foyer into the kitchen where Emma sat chatting with Ashleigh and her granddaughter Bria. Seeing them enter the room, Ashleigh rushed over to hug Sin, while shooting Beans an evil glare. Still upset by their encounter at the club, she didn't hesitate making her feelings known. He returned her look by blowing her a sarcastic kiss followed by a mocking grin. Emma turned her back to the group of men seeing them enter the room, opening the refrigerator, refusing to acknowledge Sin's presence as he stood in her kitchen admiring how big and pretty Bria had gotten. He had grown use to Emma's behavior towards him through the years and paid her no mind. Her disdain for him was no secret and although the feeling was mutual Sin wasn't one to wear his emotions on his sleeve. Out of respect for his father he hadn't displayed not even an ounce of disrespect towards her.

After a few minutes, Nate tapped Sin letting him know that they needed to get going. Marion was waiting on them in his office. The three men exited the kitchen, headed up the stairs and entered the office where they found Marion standing behind his desk looking out the window at his grandchildren playing in the pool. Seeing the group enter, he placed his glass of cognac on the desk, walked around and greeted Sin and Beans with hugs before leaning up against the front of his desk.

"Whaddup Pops," Sin said taking the seat directly in front of him. "What's all the extra men about?"

"Precautions," Marion said. "They hit the Perrucci's last night and the Brigandi's this morning," he informed his son.

"They who...the feds?" Sin asked.

"No, Di Toro and his people," he said picking up the Daily News off his desk and passing it to his son. "They killed Carlo's son right in front of his house," Marion explained. "Big Phil told me this muthafucka was planning to make a move."

Sin stared down at the headline that read: GANGLAND RETURNS. The picture was of a gruesome crime scene with the head of the family, Salvatore Perrucci, laid sprawled out in a pool of blood. Along with three members of his family, including his underboss, all victims of a well-orchestrated hit that played out in front of a Manhattan restaurant the night before.

"What about the truce amongst the Five Families?" Beans inquired as he got a look at the paper.

"It died with Carlo Brigandi." Marion stated.

"We just wanted to make you two aware of what's going on," Uncle Nate said. "We don't know which way he might come at us but we know he's coming, sooner or later."

"Probably sooner than later," Sin declared. "He's banking

on you being preoccupied with Mason and the election. Hoping he can catch you slippin'."

"You think I don't know that?" Marion asked. "I've been doing this for a long time. I done seen everything but God, boy. I'm just hoping to avoid a war long enough to get your brother elected. I don't need shit fucking that up."

"I ain't really into politics. I'm out here in these streets, and we gonna be on the front line when it all go down. I ain't trying to get caught with just my dick in my hand. No disrespect Unc," Beans explained to Marion.

"Yeah Pops, I ain't trying to be no sitting duck while we wait for Mason to get elected. I say we be proactive instead of reactive," Sin expressed.

"But I say we're gonna handle it my way." Marion declared.

"Whatever you say Pops," Sin conceded but clearly in disagreement.

Marion, noticing his face, asked Nate and Beans to step out of the room so that he could speak to his son in private. The two men got up and exited the room, closing the door behind them.

"What's going on?" Sin asked as soon as he saw the door close.

"That's what I wanna know?" Marion quizzed. "You seem to have a problem with the way I'm handling things."

"I just think—"

"It's not about what you think. It's about what I say," Marion cut him off as fast as he began to speak. "Now if you suddenly got a misconception of what's going on here, we can make other arrangements. Cuz too many kings can ruin an army. You understand me?"

"Nah, it's no problem," Sin said still upset but respecting his father's position.

"Now what's this I'm hearing about your spots getting hit out in Brooklyn? Yeah," he continued while starting to nod his head. "Nothing goes on in Brooklyn that I don't know about son. You got a lot of ideas about how I'm handling shit. You need to be handling that."

"I know," Sin admitted hating the fact that he hadn't been able to take care of the situation before he was being asked about it by his father. "I'm on it tho. I got eyes and ears in the streets. As soon as I get word of who it is, they're dead."

"Ok. I'll take your word for it. On another note, have you spoke wit' your sister about that business opportunity?"

"Yeah."

"How long do you think it will take you to get up the money to invest?" Marion inquired.

"Not long." Sin replied. "Speaking of money, I need to get back to the city and check on some."

"Understandable, I need to start getting ready for this damn campaign dinner tonight." Marion said finishing the last bit of liquor in his glass.

* * *

Emma sat at her vanity mirror admiring her timeless beauty as she brushed her hair back neatly into a classy bun. She wore her middle-aged years to perfection. She didn't need any surgical enhancements to perfect her beauty she just rehearsed her daily regimes of natural exfoliation to keep her skin tight and youthful. She kept all her natural secrets in a pad she stashed in her night table and would pass it down to her daughters. "You have to maintain your beauty if you don't want your man to stray," was one of the many things she would say to them preparing them for a long lasting marriage in the spotlight. She heard stories of Marion's indiscretions but she never cried over them. He afforded her a lifestyle that only a queen was deemed worthy of having, and she confidently wore her crown and set rules in her castle. A few of them were: "There will be no living bitch's voice heard in this house except mine" and "Love yourself enough that is makes others uncomfortable." But her favorite, and the one that she lived by was "Treat me like a queen and I'll treat you with respect. Treat me like a game and I'll show you how it's played." Emma took no shorts from anyone, demanded what was hers and without argument she ultimately got what she wanted. However, there was one thing she could not seem to exclude out of her circle and that was Yasin Kennedy. Marion would normally do anything to keep his wife happy, but when it came to Sin he more or less pacified the situation to Emma, making up for it with other things to keep her happy. Emma adjusted her robe straps tightly around her waist, sitting up in her chair and reaching for her face powder as she cringed at the thought of Sin showing his face tonight at Mason's campaign dinner. *This is for family only,* she thought, *Marion needs to relate that to his bastard trash tonight or I will be forced to.*

Mason entered his parent's suite, breaking her train of thought, wearing a blue suit white shirt and red tie. He sported 24 karat cufflinks with diamond crusts in the middle. He looked ever so much the part of a mayoral candidate. "Mom we have 20 minutes before we need to be in the limo and you don't look even half way ready," said Mason. Smiling at how clean and handsome her eldest son looked on his important night she turned around in her chair crossing one leg over the other and said, "Son, you don't worry about me. The hard part is already done with my preparation, all I have to do is slip into my dress and you will see what absolute perfection looks like in a short period of time." They both shared a smile as she got up to adjust his tie and smooth out any wrinkles or lint that may have appeared on his tailored suit. "Have you spoken to your father lately?" Emma inquired without making eye contact with Mason, just focused on his tie.

"Ah yes...I spoke with Pops this morning. As a matter of

fact we spoke about tonight's event," Mason replied. Emma now looked up at her son with disappointing eyes and walked over to her mirror to slip on her dress. "Zip me up," was all she said. Mason walked over to his mother and helped her with her dress. He knew his mother very well so he understood by her facial expression that she wasn't pleased. "Mom, I have this under control, just let me handle Pops."

"Oh do you? Emma quickly retorted. "From what it looks like to me son, you are still playing second best. Every time I turn around Sin is being summoned by your father or your Uncle Nate for a meeting...not you!"

"Once I win this election things will change Mom, trust me. I'll be able to help Pops get so many of his projects completed through my political ties. He won't see a need to run anything by anybody but me." Mason stated confidently.

"Is that what you think it's all about son? Helping your father with his political affairs? Mason honey, what we have here, what your father has built for us, our family, the Holloways... is an empire! It's going to take more than just some political maneuvering to run it. If you don't take control now everything that I have raised you to be and groomed you for will be a waste. You are the heir to this throne and if you do not grab it by the horns it will be swept from underneath your feet like yesterday's trash. And I will be damned if I let you or your father allow that piece of shit Sin to reap the benefits of what was built on this Holloway name."

Seeing the seriousness in his mother's face Mason knew he had to say something to put his mother's feelings at ease. "Mom have I ever let you down?" he asked staring in her eyes. "I got this and I promise you what is rightfully ours will remain ours."

Emma stroked the side of her son's face smiling and showing a sign of pleasure. "I am not in any way trying to pressure you darling. I just need you to understand how important this is to our family dear. Plus, I can't count on your wife to consult you when it comes to family affairs. She seems to be caught up in everything except you sometimes. But that, of course, is another story for another time," Emma snidely replied.

"Mom, look at me. I have it under control. Don't you worry your pretty little head," Mason responded sounding like his father.

"Worries...who has time for any, distractions are what they are," she replied. "Very well son. Have Diego pull the car around and I'll be down shortly."

CHAPTER 13

"Everybody get the fuck on the floor!" yelled the first masked man through the door of the brownstone waving the automatic weapon in his hand. He was followed by another man brandishing two Glock 9's, concealing his identity with a mask as well. Slim, a tall light skinned street vet, who ran a weed spot on Halsey Street and was one of Barkim's top guys, sat on the couch rolling up, while two of his workers played NBA 2k13. Startled by the sound of the door being kicked in, he spilled all the weed into his lap trying to reach for his gun that sat just out of his reach on the nearby coffee table. But it was already too late because the first gunman through the door was on him and had his weapon pressed up against his head before Slim realized what was actually going on. Using his better judgment, he pulled back his hand and joined his two workers that were already on the floor at gun point. Slim watched as the man holding the single gun paced back and forth through the house looking for a stash he knew was there. After a few brief moments, he began to grow frustrated unable to locate what they had come for. He grabbed one of Slim's workers and began striking him over the head with his gun, opening a wound on the top of his head. Blood flowed down his face onto his shirt turning it red instantly. Screaming at Slim to tell them the location of the money and drugs hidden in the house, the man aimed the gun at the worker, threatening to kill him and demanding for Slim or one of them to reveal its location. Slim didn't say a word only looking at the worker still laid next to him and giving him a look that let him know not to open his mouth either. Asking once again and receiving no answer the man fired.

BANG!

The sound rang out, echoing inside the entire room, shaking Slim up slightly and causing him to turn his head and close his eyes not wanting to see the carnage. As the ringing in his ears subsided he could hear his workers agonizing screams. Slim opened his eyes and seen that he had been shot in his thigh and laid on the ground writhing in pain as blood poured out of his wound. The gunman never broke from his mission. Grabbing the other worker off the ground, this time holding the gun to the side of his head, showing he meant business and he wanted an answer. Slim stared in the eyes of the young worker and saw nothing but fear staring back at him. He was only 16 years old, a baby. Slim had been fucking his mom off and on for years. That was why he had taken the lil' nigga under his wing and showed him how to get money. Although he didn't love the kid's mother in any sense of the word, he had enough respect for her not to want her to have to bury her son. He was out here in the streets and death was sometimes apart of the game and one day it might come for the little nigga but today wasn't going to be his day. Before the gunman could ask again Slim spoke up, informing him that he could show him where it was. The man who had been doing all the talking instructed his partner to go with Slim to retrieve the goods, reminding him to keep his eye on him at all times.

"If he moves wrong...kill em." He meanwhile stayed in the front room with his gun aimed at the two workers.

* * *

The flashing lights of the ambulance bounced off the windshield slightly impairing Det. Alvarado's vision as they pulled up directly behind it and parked. On the scene of yet another home invasion, their fifth one in two months. The detectives had grown used to the gruesome scenes the killers had left in their wake and were fully prepared for what they were about to see. *Whoever is behind these robbery homicides are some ruthless motherfuckers,* Det. Harris thought to himself, exiting the black Chevy Impala on the passenger side. The robbers truly believed in the old motto "Leave no witnesses" as no one had yet to survive one of their crimes. Entering the brownstone through the downstairs entrance, the detectives were immediately thrown off; the scene of this robbery was unlike any of the others. Despite the fresh blood that had soaked into the carpet in the living room, there weren't any bodies, only a young man who looked to be in his early twenties being attended to by paramedics for a gunshot wound to the thigh.

"Something's not right," Alvarado voiced to his partner, who he could tell by the look on his face was thinking the exact same thing. "This is not their M.O."

"My thoughts exactly," Harris replied. In all his years in homicide he had only seen somebody responsible for the types of murders being committed amplify their efforts. Surveying the crime scene, he just couldn't seem to wrap his mind around why they had gone through all the trouble of killing every witness up to now but had decide to let one live. Needing a bit more clarity, he decided to try and get some answers from the gunshot victim as he was now on the stretcher getting ready to be pushed out of the apartment.

"Hold on for just a second," he called out to the medics walking towards them. "I need to ask this one a couple of questions. What happened in here tonight?" he asked but received no answer as the victim chose not to acknowledge him. Alvarado decided to intervene. "Oh, we got ourselves a tough guy," he said amused by the young punk. "Let's see how tough he is then," the detective said looking at his partner. "What went down in here tonight?" he repeated this time leaning all of his weight directly on the leg with the gunshot.

The victim let out a blood curdling scream as pain shot all through his body. "We got robbed," he shouted hoping the detective would get off of him. It worked. Alvarado lifted his weight off of him.

"By who?" Harris quizzed.

"I don't know."

"You gotta do better than that," Harris said as Alvarado returned his weight onto the wounded leg.

"Arrrgh!" the man's scream could be heard from outside the residence. "I don't know they had on masks!" he yelled. "They came in waving guns and shit, tellin' niggas to get on the ground."

"Niggas who?" Harris asked pushing for more information.

"Me, Slim and some lil' nigga. I don't know his name," he continued.

"Weed man Slim?"

"Yeah man, get off my leg!" he cried and pleaded. Alvarado eased up as the young man continued providing them with details. "That's the crazy part, they came in looking for some bricks. And that's what they left with."

"Slim is the weed man. He jumping in the cocaine business now?" Harris said looking at his partner trying to make sense of it all.

"Nah," the young man replied. "I heard him talking earlier on the phone, he was holding them for some nigga named Barkim."

"You sure?" Alvarado asked leaning on his wound again for kicks.

"Yeah!" he screamed.

"Get him out of here," Harris said before turning his attention to his partner. The name Barkim had peaked both detectives' interest; they were very familiar with the name. He was a member of Sin's crew, which meant this somehow involved the big fish they had been hunting. They immediately knew they needed to find Slim and put the pressure on him to cooperate. They would get Sin even if they had to climb the ladder up to him slowly.

CHAPTER 14

The moans of a woman being pleasured could vaguely be heard over the Trey Songz CD providing the soundtrack for the sex session taking place inside the bedroom. London, a thick redbone with ass for days, laid on her back with her eyes closed and her legs spread open, rubbing one hand back and forth across her breast teasing her hard nipples. Using her free hand, she gripped the back of her mate's head pushing his face and tongue deeper inside of her. He flicked his tongue at a rapid but steady pace, savoring every drop of her juices as he tasted her. London's body moved like a snake as she moved her hips, enjoying his oral skills. Replacing his tongue with his two fingers, her moans elevated as he began sucking on her clit and using his fingers to massage her g-spot, sending tingles racing all through her body. London could feel her climax building and instructed for him to suck on her clit harder and he did as she requested. He was so orally gifted and had her legs feeling like jelly as he continued to please her. London reached for the pillow on the side of her, placing it over her face as she screamed into it and began biting down on it when she heard a loud noise.

Quickly removing the pillow from her face, she seen blood everywhere as the man that was just pleasing her lay lifeless between her legs with the back of his head missing. London screamed at the horrific sight of her legs, hands, and sheets covered in his blood. Looking up, she saw two men standing in her bedroom, both with their weapons pointed at her. She immediately knew who they were and who they were looking for.

"Now that I got your attention," Sin said with his gun still smoking. "Where's ya brother?"

Still shaking from the sight of the dead man between her legs, London tried to compose herself and keep her emotions in. Sin's words didn't immediately register as she had so many thoughts racing through her mind. How the fuck did they get in? was her first followed by, I'm always in some shit behind this nigga, referring to her brother, who she hadn't seen in days.

"You heard what the man asked you sweetheart?" Sheik said calmly.

"I don't know where my brother is. I haven't seen or talked to him in days," she replied still shaking like a leaf.

"Yeah?" Sin questioned not believing a word she said.

"Yeah," she replied. "And I ain't got shit to do with whatever my brother got going on. So I would appreciate it if y'all were to get the fuck outta my house."

Sin inched closer to the bed causing her to scoot back and pull the covers up attempting to cover her naked body. "This ain't that type of party ma," he said finding humor in her thinking he was going to attempt to rape her. He walked around the side of the bed and picked up her handbag off the nightstand, searching through it until he found her phone. Scrolling down her call log he spotted her brother's number, checking the date and time, she had been telling the truth. He pressed the screen dialing the number, putting the phone to his ear as it rang. Allowing it to ring until the voice mail picked up, he hung up and immediately dialed again. After still getting no answer he hung up and tossed the phone on the bed.

"When you speak to your brother, cuz I know you will. Tell him we stopped by and if he don't come see me I'll be back."

"Why?" she asked as tears ran down her face. "I ain't got nothing to do with this."

"Then you better make sure he come see me." Sin said before exiting along with Sheik.

* * *

Ashleigh sat in the back of the Lincoln town car heading

towards Case's house. They had been seeing each other on and off for a few weeks now and she enjoyed hanging out with him. Although he wasn't the type of dude she would normally deal with, she liked his style and his take charge demeanor. His thuggish ways and boss attitude turned her on and made her pussy tingle. Tonight, she planned on showing him how much she liked being around him. She even decided to go to his hood to see him instead of taking him up on his offer to get a room at the Waldorf in the city. In her own way, she was trying to show him that she wasn't a stuck up prissy chick that was scared to come to the hood.

The driver pulled up to a brownstone in Harlem and parked. Ashleigh reached in her bag and pulled out her iPhone sending a text to Case's phone letting him know she was downstairs. She peeped the surroundings of the neighborhood she was in and saw the late night hustlers getting their last little bit of money on the corner as the fiends circled the block. A few people were in the line at the corner store laughing at the drunk man singing loudly, while the hustlers cursed at him telling him to keep it moving. She was interrupted from her sightseeing by the message alert; it was Case replying to her.

"Get out the car, you scared Hollywood?"

Ashleigh smiled to herself as she read it and replied.

Tuh! Are you serious! Never scared just wanted to let you know I was here. Now come open the door.

Ashleigh was always privileged as she never had to experience the hood. Marion made it his business to keep her in the best of neighborhoods growing up. If he knew she was rendezvousing through Harlem World in the middle of the night, he would definitely have something to say. Ashleigh opened the door to exit the vehicle.

"Thank you Rick have a goodnight," she told the driver.

"Do you want me to wait for you Ms. Ashleigh?" Rick replied.

"No I'm good," she said flashing him a smile. Ashleigh grabbed her clutch and shut the door behind her. When she looked up, she saw Case holding one of the double doors open awaiting her to come up the stairs. Ashleigh immediately began to smile at the sight of the sexy brown skinned thug posted up wearing some basketball shorts, Nike slide in flip flops and a wife beater. Her pussy began to tingle at the thought of her straddling him. She was most definitely turned on by Case and planned on letting him know how much she was.

"Took you long enough," Case said.

"Patience is a virtue," she said as she walked passed him and up the stairs. Ashleigh made sure she strutted up every stair, letting her dress rise and never trying to pull it down so that Case could get a glance at the nothing she wore underneath.

"Yo, you ain't got no draws on?" said a surprised Case.

140

"Underwear are overrated," she replied nonchalantly.

"Word, I feel that," he said with a smirk on his face. Ashleigh headed straight to his bedroom and put her jacket on his bed. Case watched her move through his crib like she was familiar and comfortable, shaking his head and chuckling at her moves. *This ma'fucka here. She always trying to be the boss of something or someone. I like her fucking ass.*

Ashleigh wore an all-black sundress with spaghetti straps and her hair in a bun. She stood in front of the mirror on the dresser and let down her hair, running her fingers through it.

Case stood behind her and began to run his fingers through her hair as well and kissed her on her shoulders. "You know you not leaving here until I taste you right?"

"Is that right?" replied Ashleigh,

"You better believe it."

"Well, I wouldn't have it any other way"

Case pulled the straps of her dress down and let her dress fall to the floor. Ashleigh wore nothing but her birthday suit in front of the mirror. Not only did she not wear any panties she conveniently forgot her bra as well. Her C cup breasts stood up firmly and her nipples were at attention. Case palmed her breasts from behind and bit softly on her shoulder sending all types of electricity to Ashleigh's body. She closed her eyes and let her head fall back enjoying Case fondling her. Instantly, his dick hardened rubbing up against her ass. He turned her around, picked her up and sat her on his dresser.

Ashleigh opened her legs without hesitation giving him a nice view of her juice box. Case bit down on his lip staring at her pretty shaved pussy parting open. Ashleigh's clit was glistening and he wanted to taste her. He went to dive in head first but she stopped him.

"Mmm, I want to feel it first," she requested with a soft moan.

Case wasted no time and stuck his now throbbing dick into her, palming her ass tightly and gave her hard thrusts as her moans grew louder. He worked her walls as she dug her nails into his back until he felt her explode. Then he went down and licked up all of her juices. Ashleigh was enjoying every bit of what he was giving her and planned on spending the rest of her night enjoying him. After feasting on her for a little while, Case picked her up and headed to the bed.

"Damn you giving it up like that," was all she could say to him.

"I ain't even start yet," he bragged.

Case and Ashleigh sexed for hours, cumming multiple times until they both collapsed onto the bed. They both laid next to each other contemplating if they had the energy to go another round.

CHAPTER 15

The sounds of the latest Meek Mill's CD filled the car as Sin navigated his Jaguar through the streets of Brooklyn late at night. After receiving a call from Marion earlier informing him that Stefano Greco, a close ally and member of the Catanzano family, had been gunned down in his car, he knew that it was only a matter of time before their organization would be dragged into the ongoing war between the "Five Families". Mike Di Toro was slaughtering the other families at an alarming rate and was slowly taking control of the city. At the same time, he was waging war on law enforcement in order to prevent any chances of investigations or prosecutions. Iron Mike wanted to be boss of all bosses; something the New York Mafia hadn't seen since the 30's. If that happened he could dictate who could and couldn't get money, something Sin wasn't willing to leave to chance.

His phone began to light up the inside of the car

indicating it was ringing. Picking it up to see who it was, he saw Ariane's name and number and put the phone back down. He had been avoiding her calls as of late and had barely spoken with her since spending the night with her. He still had the same strong feeling about her, but with all the turmoil going on around him he knew he needed to be focused on business. She was a beautiful distraction but a distraction nonetheless.

Sin pulled up and parked in front of the barber shop on Willoughby. His fresh pair of timberland boots hit the ground first, untied with the tongues flipped down, as he stepped out of his vehicle dressed in a denim jacket and matching jeans, with a fitted white t-shirt underneath and a Yankee's fitted hat. His yellow gold Cuban link chain swung back and forth as he walked around the front of the car with his signature strut and stepped up onto the sidewalk. Hopping out of the passenger side alongside of him was the young gunner Kyrie. Surveying the block up and down, Sin proceeded towards the door after being satisfied in what he saw. Posted in front of the door of the shop stood a group of teenagers ranging in different ages; the youngest looked to be no older than fourteen. He was the first one Sin recognized as the two men approached the group.

"Wassup boy, whatchu doin' out here this late?" Sin asked the youngster.

"Yo wassup Sin," the young boy replied turning seeing Sin. "You know what it is. I'm just out here trying to get it," he said before extending his hand for dap.

"Yeah..." Sin said giving the young boy a crazy look as he dapped him up.

"What's good Sin?" another one of the teenage boys spoke. "That ride is crazy. You should let me whip that shit one day."

Sin just laughed as he reached in his pocket and pulled out a knot of money. "You don't wanna whip the next man's shit, you wanna whip ya own." Sin schooled him while peeling a couple of hundreds off the top of the stack and handing one to each teen out there. This was something he had done regularly; Sin always showed love to the hood. It was why he was so revered in the streets.

"Let me talk to you for a second," Sin said turning his attention back to the youngest member of the group, motioning for him to take a walk with him. Kyrie kept an eye on the rest of the group with his hand not too far from the gun he had tucked on him. With so much shit popping off he was on edge like his boss and though they were just teenage kids he didn't put shit past them. He wasn't that much older than them and could remember putting in some work for Sin when he was around their age. Plus, none of them looked familiar to him.

After making it a couple of feet from the group, just enough so they were out of ear range, Sin turned to the young man. "Now I'ma ask you again what you doing out here this late? And don't hit me with that 'out here tryin' to get it bullshit,' cuz we both know better," he said speaking in a more serious tone.

"Nah for real, I was just out here with my friends walking around. We wasn't doin' nothing I promise," the young man confessed.

"Don't you got school in the morning? And I know your grandmother don't know you out here. Take ya ass home now and don't let me catch you out here no more. You feel me?" Sin said as he peeled a few more bills off his knot and handed it to the young kid. "Give that to your grams and tell her you seen me at the store or sumthin' and I'll be through to see her soon."

Sin then watched as the boy collected his crew and walked off. He was the smallest out the bunch but a born leader. To Sin it was all too familiar, he knew exactly where the kid got those traits from, even if the boy didn't.

"Yo, what was that about?" a curious Kyrie asked after watching him interact with the kid. "Who dat lil nigga?" he motioned as the group disappeared around the corner.

"Somebody I promised I'd look out for," he answered, not willing to give up much more information than that as he opened the door to the barber shop and walked in.

The Chop Shop, as it was called, was empty except for the owner; a pudgy middle aged man named Chop, short for Pork Chop, sweeping up the place. It was his daily routine at closing time. Chop was a well-respected businessman in the hood. He had owned the barber shop on Willoughby for many years, dating back to when Sin was younger. But what looked on the surface to be a just your regular local barber shop was much more than meets the eye. For years Chop had been running the biggest after hour gambling spot in Brooklyn right out of the basement of the shop. Set up like a mini casino with dealers and scantily clad cocktail waitresses serving drinks, the spot housed crap tables, black jack tables and the biggest poker game in town. It was a stick up kid's dream but the security system was tighter than a military fort and if that wasn't enough to keep thieves at bay, Chop was never more than an arm's length away from a weapon. Seeing Sin and his protégé enter, he stopped sweeping and placed his broom up against the wall.

"What's good Chop?" Sin said greeting the man.

"It's your world youngster," he replied removing the cigarette from his mouth and blowing out a cloud of smoke. "If I had your hands, I'd cut mines off."

"I hear that hot shit," Sin said giving Chop a pound and a hug. "I appreciate you makin' dat call tho." Sin continued.

"I told you I would as soon as I heard something," Chop reminded him.

"Yeah, yeah, most definitely," Sin said nodding his head. "That's love."

"Yeah but I don't deal in feelings, I deal in millions," the chubby man stated returning his cigarette to his mouth with his right hand and rubbing his fingers together on his left, reminding Sin about their financial agreement.

"Same ol' Chop," Sin said with a smile while reaching in his pocket.

Descending the steps of the shop and entering the dimly light casino area, which was void of any patrons, a very unfamiliar scene for the spot but it was the least of Sin's concerns. Business had been halted in order for him to deal with a glaring issue within his organization. Making his way through the quiet main area into the back room with Kyrie a half step behind him, he began hearing voices. Now, standing in the entry way, he could finally see Beans standing in front of a pool table surrounded by Barkim, Ali and Sheik. The men were standing over a bloody and battered man who was tied up on top of it. Approaching the pool table Sin noticed the man's shirt had been ripped open and he had large gashes across his chest, the result of the electric circular saw resting beside him. His eyes were swollen shut and he cried in agony while pleading with Beans to let him go.

"Damn Slim," Sin said calling the man by his name, causing him to begin pleading his case to Sin upon hearing his voice in the room. Sin, like the two detectives at the scene of the last robbery, had quickly put two and two together as well. He realized that there weren't any similarities to the previous home invasions that had occurred. Mainly the fact that there were witnesses left not only alive but basically unharmed. Even the gunshot wound had turned out to be nothing more than a flesh wound. His suspicions were confirmed when Slim went missing right after the robbery and then popped up in the Bronx a few weeks later trying to get the large amount of bricks off to an old Dominican friend of Chop's, who had gotten the word out about Slim and the missing work. Choosing to make a powerful connect over a quick buck the man placed the called to Chop, who relayed Slim's whereabouts to Sin.

"Please Sin," he begged unable to see, just looking in the direction of where the voice had come from. "Don't do me like this."

"Don't do you like what nigga?" Sin asked as he removed his jacket and picked up the saw off the pool table. "Fuck I ever did to you besides show you love my nigga? How you gonna steal from me?" Sin questioned as he fired up the machine and began cutting into Slim's wrist until he had severed his hand from the rest of him.

The loud cry echoed throughout the room, causing some of them to turn away, as blood squirted everywhere from what once was Slim's hand. "Please...Please Sin, Please just let me go man!" he begged for mercy.

"Nah nigga, that ain't how this works," Sin said turning off the saw, putting it down and removing his gun from his waist. Hearing the gun being cocked, Slim resorted to call out for the Lord to help him. "Then you tried moving the work in the same city? How stupid could you be?" Sin asked.

"I don't know what you talking 'bout, it wasn't me..." Slim tried explaining but received a shot in his knee, causing him to scream in excruciating pain.

"C'mon my nigga don't insult my intelligence. Admit to what you've done and we can get this over with. If not I'ma reload this muthafucka and potshot you all night. It's up to you."

Already in unbearable pain, the thought of enduring more became too much for Slim. "Ok, Ok, it was me. I did it!" he finally screamed out with spit and blood oozing from his mouth.

"Why my nigga? We was family. Bricks and bales, it was dat simple...everybody eating."

"Eating off ya plate!" Slim grunted out through his pain and clenched teeth. "What kind of nigga don't wanna be his own boss," he stated seemingly finding the courage knowing he wasn't going to make it out of this situation alive anyway. He was older than every man in the room and had grown tired of being an underling, so when he saw what he perceived as his chance at a big lick, he took it. He devised a plan to stage a robbery, with the hopes that suspicion would fall on the crew who was really doing the home invasions. Everything would have gone smoothly if his out of town buyer hadn't fallen through leaving him scrambling and ending up in the

Bronx trying to sell them. "That's what you need to ask yourself. You crazy if you think these niggas standing next to you wouldn't put a bullet in your head to wear your crown." Slim continued. "I saw my shot and I took it."

Sin just stared down at him as the room fell silent for a moment. Honestly he understood exactly where Slim was coming from; after all he had once felt that way. But understanding didn't mean sympathy and it damn sure didn't translate into mercy. "Let me ask you something," he stated while pointing his gun directly at Slim. "Who else helped you?" Hoping that if there were any more snakes in his yard, he would reveal them.

"That's something you gotta figure out on your own. I ain't no snitch," he proclaimed.

"And I respect that." Sin replied to the last words he would ever speak then squeezed off two rounds. The first shot ripped through Slim's throat and the second hit him square in the forehead, killing him instantly.

CHAPTER 16

Ariane was in such a good sleep that it took her a minute to realize that the doorbell she kept hearing was real and not part of the dream she was currently enjoying. Finally opening her eyes, she quickly jumped out of bed, dressed in a pink cami and short set by Victoria's Secret and slid on her slippers. Swiftly walking down the hallway unaware of how long the person had been ringing, she made it to the door in mere seconds. "Just a minute," she called out not wanting the person to leave before she was able to answer the door. "Who is it?" she called out once again.

"Delivery," the man on the other side of the door replied.

Ariane looked through the peephole unsure if he was at the right address. When she saw a short and burly, not so handsome white man holding a single long stemmed white rose and a white card. I know he didn't, she thought to herself, realizing that this must be one of Sin's stunts. But the way he had avoided her after they had sex, she was through with him. Not that she felt stupid for having sex with him because she didn't, it was because she had tricked herself into believing that he was different. Ariane was angry with herself more than she was at him, after all she knew better. She had only been calling him as of late to return the Range Rover he had left her in possession of. Wanting to make sure she was right about it being him she asked the delivery man who it was from. Her suspicions were confirmed by his answer.

"A Mr. Yasin Kennedy," he said reading the card.

Ariane shook her head, "Predictable", she thought. Typical nigga shit. All his 'that ain't me ma' shit, fuck outta here. She wanted to open the door and tell the man where he could stick that rose, but decided against it as he was just the messenger. Opening the door, the gentleman handed her the white rose and the card and offered a smile, she half-heartedly returned the gesture. The card simply read: I'm sorry...here's to new beginnings. She found the gesture no way near suitable, and she had a message of her own she wanted to give the delivery man to return with. But before she could say anything her mouth dropped as the man stepped aside and she saw a sea of white roses and close to ten delivery men marching up her steps, each holding what looked to be 50 roses in their hands. She held the door open in amazement as each man made multiple trips in and out of her house until her living room was half filled with roses. When they were finished, she closed her front door, leaned her back against it, staring at the floral shop that now sat in her living room. The roses where beautiful, but in typical Ariane fashion she had to find something to say. "I mean he coulda went with pink, but it's nice," she said under her breath. Ariane felt a knock on the door, turning to look through the peephole again, she saw the same short and burly delivery man. But this time he wasn't holding anything. Ariane assumed he must have dropped or forgotten something so she opened the door. When she did she saw the same group of delivery men marching back up her steps this time with 50 pink roses in each of their hands prepared to repeat the same process. Ariane couldn't help but smile. She had never had anyone do anything like this for her before and although she remained upset, she had to admit it was flattering. She watched as the men filled up the other half of her living room with the pink flowers leaving only a small path to walk. When they finished, Ariane asked the man who had knocked on the door if she could tip him, but he declined, telling her they had already been taken care of very handsomely then wished her a good day on his way out the door.

The sea of pink and white in her living room was beautiful; Sin had truly out done himself. Suddenly, her phone began to ring on the breakfast bar. Walking over to retrieve it she saw a familiar number. Trying her best to contain the smile on her face, she answered and tried her best to still sound upset. "What?"

"Hello Ariane," Sin said in his sexy voice that had a slight raspiness to it.

"Who is this?" she questioned sarcastically, knowing she knew that voice anywhere.

Sin ignored her sarcasm and continued. "You accept my apology?" he asked.

"No I told you before I can't be bought," she reminded him. "I can buy my own material things."

"I respect that, but I like doing nice things for you," he said just as there was another knock on the door. "You might wanna get that," he informed her.

"Ok, Sin, I forgive you!" she yelled into the phone. "No more roses, I don't have anywhere else to put them," she jokingly said opening the door.

This time the delivery man was a little taller and darker and a lot sexier. Sin stood in the door wearing a NY Giants fitted hat, khaki cargo shorts and a white t-shirt that hugged him slightly, showing off his athletic build with a gold chain and Jesus piece hanging from it. Both of his arms were stretched out and in each hand he held a Birkin bag, one white, one pink. With a smile across his face he charmingly said, "Make up bags."

Ariane pulled him in the house by his shirt and push the door closed behind him. Sin attempted to kiss her but she moved her face. "I can't stand you," she said.

"I know, I'm sorry, I got caught up handling business," he explained. "It won't happen again."

"Business? What kind of business?" she asked while grabbing his dick through his shorts and squeezing it. "This kind of business?" she asked.

"Nah ma," he said finally kissing her only to have her softly but firmly bite down on his bottom lip. "Ssss," he said from the slight pain.

"You sure?" she asked now beginning to suck on his lips while still squeezing his dick.

Sin pulled her by the hair and began tongue kissing her aggressively. Ariane bit down on his lip once again this time a little harder than before. Sin grabbed her by the neck, roughly pushing her up against the wall, then pulled her cami off her shoulders letting it fall until it rested around her waist. He began sucking on her exposed breasts, moving his tongue in a circular motion over her hard nipples. Sticking his hand inside her shorts, he slid it down until his fingers were on her clit then started rubbing it. First slowly, then picking up the pace as he heard her soft moans and felt her breath on his ear and then her warm mouth as she sucked on his earlobe. "You still mad at me?" he whispered in her ear while slipping his fingers into her soaked love box. Her wetness could be heard as he moved his fingers in and out of her steadily and Ariane's breathing became heavier as she spread her legs wider allowing him to go deeper.

"Yeeeesss!" she screamed as he caressed her g-spot until she exploded, drowning his finger in her juices. Her body shook uncontrollably and her legs felt weak as she lay against the wall. Sin placed his hands beneath her plump ass and lifted her off her feet. She wrapped her legs around him and they passionately kissed as he carried her into the living room, placing her down on the floor surrounded by roses on both sides.

Ariane sat up as he stood over her, tugging at his shorts until they fell to the floor. Reaching inside his boxer briefs she released his swollen manhood and took him into her mouth. The warmth of her mouth felt so good gliding up and down on his dick. Ariane rubbed his testicles as she glazed his rock hard penis. Turned on by his soft moans, she placed her hands inside of her shorts and played with herself, unable to wait for him the enter her.

Sin pulled back and joined her on the floor, quickly removing her shorts as he placed both her legs on his shoulders and placed himself inside of her. Ariane exploded again, arching her back off the floor as he dug deep inside her, showing her lotus flower no mercy as he pounded her body into sexual submission. Her loud screams of pure pleasure were all the fuel he needed to keep going until he felt himself ready to release. After a few more thrusts, Sin let his load off inside of her and collapsed on the floor next to her. The two of them laid there sweaty and sticky, exhausted from their passionate episode.

Slowly regaining control of her breathing, Ariane rolled over facing Sin. Looking at the ruggedly beautiful man beside her she wanted nothing more than to be his. But she needed to know something in order for her to give in completely to her feelings.

"Sin can I trust you?" she asked softly, capturing his attention.

"No doubt," he answered meaning it whole heartedly.

"I mean can I really trust you...with my fears, my pain and most importantly my heart?" she asked speaking from deep inside.

"Yes Ariane, you can trust me with all of you."

"You remember on our first date you asked me why I had moved to New York," she said her heart quickening, knowing she was about to let this man in on the biggest heartache of her life, something that still haunted her to this day. She proceeded to tell him her life story. How her mother had become a violent alcoholic after her father left them for another woman and a new family. She would take her frustrations out on them, especially Quan because he resembled their father so much. She told how he would take the blame for things, knowing he would be severely punished just to protect her from the wrath of their mom who reeked of vodka daily. Eventually, they ran away and Quan started selling drugs to make sure they were able to survive. He became good at it and ascended to one of the biggest hustlers in the DMV.

Tears began streaming from her eyes as she recalled the circumstances that led to his death. A rival hustler who was a few years old than Quan, but not as successful, had become jealous of him and the moves that he was making around the city. Unable to get at Quan in the streets, he decided to get to him another way through her. One night she and Faye went to a club in DC, something Ariane rarely did but had gone with her friend against her better judgment. As they partied an unfamiliar face in the crowd made his way over to them, trying to engage Ariane in a conversation. After several failed attempts, he became aggressively disrespectful after she turned him down. Chalking it up to his drunkenness she paid it no mind, even sharing a laugh about it with Faye. Her laughter only seemed to fuel his fire as the situation escalated rapidly. After spitting in Faye's face, the man slapped and choked Ariane right in the middle of VIP as she tried to intervene. Storming out the club, she did what she had her whole life anytime somebody of the opposite sex violated her, called Quan. Answering the phone hearing his sister in tears, he jumped out of bed, grabbed his gun and rode out to the club solo. Nobody disrespected his sister, he thought and nobody had up until then. Niggas knew better; Quan's rep in the street was strong. He was notorious for letting his gun bark.

Pulling up just as the club was letting out, Ariane and

Faye hoped into his car still a little shaken by the event that happened inside the club. Seeing his sister's tears had him drunk with anger as he waited to see the man that had put his hands on her exit the club. Ariane spotted him and quickly pointed him out to her brother. "That's him right there."

Quan lifted the gun off his lap, cocked it and jumped out the car heading straight towards the unsuspecting man. As he made it to the middle of the street, the girls noticed the doors of two parked cars open and five men jump out carrying weapons. Hearing his name being called from behind him, Quan turned to see who it was. Ambushed, he never stood a chance; the five men opened fire, filling him with bullets and leaving him a bloody mess in the street. The whole encounter in the club had been a set up. They knew Quan would come to his sister's rescue, it had been his weakness since their younger days and it had finally caught up to him.

Ariane jumped out the car screaming as she raced over to where her brother laid with his life leaking out on to the pavement beneath him. Quan gurgled and choked on his own blood as it bubbled in his mouth leaving him unable to speak. Ariane screamed for someone to help and call 911 but club goers decided that what had happened was none of their business and cleared out before cops could arrive, not wanting to answer any questions. Ariane held her brother in her arms, crying for him to hold on until paramedics arrived. But it was too late, by the time they showed up Quan's life had already expired.

Ariane expressed to Sin that was her reasoning for never wanting to deal with a guy involved in the drug game. She had seen the worst end of it and didn't wish to put her heart through that again. She was totally against the life.

Sin listened to her story and felt her pain. He too had lost the closest person to him once upon a time and knew what she was going through. He held her in his arms as she cried, occasionally running his fingers through her hair and kissing her on her forehead. Ariane snuggled up under him, finally able to stop crying as she found comfort in the sound of his heart beating in his chest. Listening, she realized that their rhythms were identical. Right then she decided she would love him for as long as he allowed her to and placed her faith in him that he would do the same.

CHAPTER 17

Barkim sat handcuffed to the chair inside an interrogation room trying to maneuver himself into a comfortable position. It had been almost five hours since he had been placed in the room and left alone. Nobody had even stuck their head into the room to check on him and he was freezing. The detectives had put the A/C on blast and the frigid temperature had not allowed him to take a nap while he waited. Finally, he found himself a comfortable spot and allowed his heavy eyes to close as he rested his head on the table in front of him. Laying there for no more than 30 seconds, he heard the door open and detectives Alvarado and Harris strutted through the door. Barkim lifted his head, thinking to himself how their timing was a little too perfect, and he was right. They had been watching him the entire time on the monitor. As soon as he got cozy and tried to rest, they came in to conduct their interview.

The two cops sat across from him placed a folder on the table. Flipping it open, Harris removed a few pictures and lined them up in front of him. Barkim leaned back in the chair refusing to look down at the pictures as the detectives stared at him for a moment without saying a word.

Finally, Alvarado spoke. "You know what those are?" he asked, pausing to see if he got a response but received none. "Those my friend are first class tickets for you; one way to death row."

Barkim remained emotionless. He knew New York didn't seek death sentences at the state level and since they were NYPD and not the feds, Alvarado's threats were hollow. Barkim was no stranger to the law and he was no dummy either.

"Look at the damn pictures," Harris shouted. "That's your boy Slim. We found his body a few days ago," he revealed. "He was tortured before he was killed. Seems like somebody had a real ax to grind with him."

Barkim's face still hadn't changed one bit. He wasn't about to give them nothing to go on.

"We know his spot got robbed a few weeks ago, and a witness tells us that the work that got stolen belonged to you. Now we know that you're really a nobody ass nigga and you take all your orders from Sin. So we figured those drugs belonged to him, correct?" Harris inquired but once again received no response.

"We also figured that this," he said pointing to the pictures on the table. "Was a result of that. Now we don't care if Sin did this or if he ordered you to. We don't want you, we want him. So all you have to do is say he was responsible and we'll make sure you never see the inside of a jail cell for this," Alvarado offered.

"Now if you don't help us, we'll put the word out that you did and you'll end up just like Slim here." Harris insisted.

The men were interrupted by the sound of the door opening. Turning to see who it was, they saw their Captain enter the room followed by a middle aged brown skinned man with a low haircut with hints of grey in it. He was void of emotion as well as any facial hair and wearing a dark grey suit.

"We have to turn him loose gentlemen," Captain Gourdine informed the two detectives.

"What do you mean Cap?" Alvarado asked with fire in his tone.

"This gentleman is free to go," he reiterated.

"Are you fucking serious?" an infuriated Harris spat, banging both of his hands on the table. "I hate these fucking guys and their high price lawyers.

"This isn't over by a long shot muthafucka," Alvarado said as he uncuffed Barkim.

"You gentlemen have a nice day," Barkim replied with a smile before exiting the interrogation room.

Barkim stepped onto the elevator happy to be going free.

As the doors begin to close, he saw a hand come through the doors causing them to re-open. The man who entered calmly pressed the button for the lobby but just as they started to move he hit the emergency stop, leaving the two men suspended between floors.

"What the fuck are you doing?" Special Agent Mosley grabbed Barkim by the shirt slamming him up against the wall pushing his gun underneath his chin. "Are you dumb or stupid? You're supposed to be getting me information on Marion Holloway not getting yourself arrested for murder. Where the fuck is my evidence?"

"I'm trying," Barkim insisted. "Sin only brings Beans around his pops. He won't bring the rest of us around him or him around us. I'm trying I swear. I just need some more time."

"Try harder," Mosley demanded pushing his gun further up into his chin. "I don't need anyone finding out you're cooperating with the government, so keep your ass out of places like this or I will personally let Marion and Sin know our little secret. Understand me?" he asked.

"Yeah." Barkim said knowing that he was in way over his head. He had gotten jammed up and decided to help the feds build a case against his longtime friend and his father. He felt guilty but it came down to him or them and he had made his choice and he knew there was no turning back now.

Mosley lowered his weapon and put it away then hit the

button allowing the elevator to start moving again. As the doors opened on the lobby floor he sarcastically said, "Now get the fuck outta my sight," before continuing his descend.

How fitting, Barkim thought to himself, realizing he had truly made a deal with the devil.

CHAPTER 18

"If you're sitting here tonight, it means you want answers. You're here on your own time because you care about this city—and you want to make sure I care about it as much as you do. You want to make sure I'll bring real solutions with me to office, not just bandages. The Office of Mayor should be held by an individual who can actually bring solutions that will change this city for the better. New York needs a drastic new approach before it's too late. If we do things the way they've always been done, then things will remain the way they've always been. And that, at this point, means a continued decline in the quality of life and an increase in crime. Mayor Mahoney has not met the standards set forth by the great people of this city and that is a gross negligence and completely unacceptable. Don't let it get any worse, let's not let this city go another year at the bottom of the totem pole. If you elect me as your next mayor, I will serve this city and the needs of its most precious and valuable resource, the people. Vote Mason Holloway this coming Election Day, and help usher in a promising new future for New York City."

The crowd in the town hall rose to their feet applauding Mason's inspiring words. He had always been great at delivering speeches. It was a quality that helped him well in his rise up the political ranks. He understood the importance of tonight's speech with the election only a few weeks away, and the polls being the way they were, most showing him slightly behind. He needed to nail it if he had any hopes of gaining ground, and he did. Looking down at the front row he could see smiles on the faces of every member of the Holloway family who had come out in full strength to show their support. The biggest smiles belonging to Marion and Emma, but for different reasons. Emma was happy to see her son looking strong and in command. She felt her talk with him had really hit home and it was apparent to her in the way he stood on that stage looking like the next leader of not only the city but of the family as well. Marion enjoyed seeing his plans coming together, having a Holloway strolling the halls of 260 Broadway as the head of the city would be a constant reminder of how far he had brought his family. And it would serve as his biggest weapon in his arsenal. On the verge of an all-out war, Marion knew the power of political connections were stronger than twenty regimes.

Mason was met by his beautiful wife Khari and their

children upon exiting the stage. She placed a kiss on his lips and she beamed with excitement. Next to greet him was Ashleigh, followed by Cassie, Elijah, and Jewlz then Uncle Nate. Emma kissed him on the cheek and whispered in his ear how proud of him she was. That meant a lot to him but the look of approval on his father's face, as he extended his hand for a firm shake, was worth all of their well wishes and congratulations combined.

"You're on your way son. That was a compelling speech you gave. You should be proud of yourself win or lose," Marion said.

"But of course we're gonna win." Emma intervened.

"Of course." Marion said with the smile that had captivated her all those years ago. He was just as sexy to her now as he was then. Starting from nothing he had amassed power, prestige and a fortune and she had rode shotgun as he built a legacy that would forever be attached to their name. After a few minutes of brief conversation Marion informed the group that he had secured a private room for them to dine at Philippe's, so they were able to continue celebrating Mason's wonderful night.

"I'm gonna have to miss this one," Ashleigh announced to everyone's disappointment. "I have somewhere to be."

"And where might that be?" Cassie asked.

"None-ya," Ashleigh said as she made her rounds kissing everyone before heading off.

His father's announcement made Mason smile widen, the fact that he had made reservations showed that he had confidence that Mason was going to do great. He placed his arms around Khari and squeezed her tight, admiring how elegant she looked in her dress. He couldn't wait to be alone with her later that evening.

Uncle Nate, along with a few members of Marion's security force, began ushering the family out of the venue's private exit into their waiting vehicles. Emma, still deeply delighted with Mason's performance, couldn't stop singing his praises as they all spilled from the doors of the event. Cassie and Elijah's vehicle was first to pull up and they along with Cassie's two boys jumped in the car. MJ, Mason's son, begged to ride with his aunt and big cousins. Cassie had no problem with his request and allowed him to join them.

Mason and Khari's ride pulled up next followed by Marion and Emma's. Emma, engaged in deep conversation with her son, motioned to her husband that she was going to ride with Mason, Khari and Bria. Marion nodded and slid into the black and grey Rolls Royce along with Nate.

The line of cars exited slowly through the parking lot, navigating through the orange cones that had been placed down by police officers working the event. Approaching a uniformed officer standing in the middle of the street with a whistle in his mouth directing the flow of traffic, the line of cars began to slow up, only to have him motion for them to keep moving, all but the Ghost transporting Marion. Surprisingly he blew his whistle and held his hand up indicating for them to stop. The driver slammed on the brakes causing Marion and Nate to jerk forward. Nate immediately began cursing the cop out, even though the windows were up and his foul language could only be heard by the men in the car. Seeing the frustration on their faces, the cop gave a sly grin just as a group of men emerged seemingly from nowhere armed with automatic weapons, and opened fire on the car, turning the luxury vehicle into a quarter million dollar block of swiss cheese.

* * *

Mason was in heaven listening to his mother showering him with praises, unaware that his father's car hadn't made the turn at the light with them. It wasn't until they heard the shots that they knew something was wrong. Emma began to scream at the driver to stop the car and turn around, as the joyous mood inside the vehicle quickly shifted into panic and fear. She needed visual confirmation of what her heart was telling her had just happened.

Mason was at a loss for words as he watched the faces of his wife and daughter fill up with fear. Finally, he yelled for the driver to stop the car and do what his mother had instructed. The SUV came to a screeching halt in the middle of the street catching everyone off guard. But more surprising was that the driver didn't move the car another inch.

Emma screamed again for him to turn the car around and head back towards where the shots had been fired, but her orders seemed to fall on deaf ears. A loud shot rang out inside the truck.

BANG!

The head of the security member seated in the passenger side next to the driver instantly exploded from the impact of the bullet as his brains painted the passenger side window bloody red. Khari screamed at the top of her lungs at the sickening sight of the man's head bursting, quickly grabbing Bria and covering her eyes. The driver then turned his gun on the group in the backseat as Mason threw his hands up over his face hoping not to get shot. All the confidence he showed only minutes ago on the stage were gone as he shook like a leaf at the mercy of the gun wielding driver.

"My husband will have your head for this," Emma said bravely.

"Your husband is dead lady," the man said in a menacing tone, his words piercing Emma's soul.

The back door of the SUV jerked open and another man waving a gun was there to greet the frightened family. Reaching into the vehicle he grabbed hold of Bria and began a tug of war with Khari, who had a death grip on her daughter and was not willing to let her go. Mason yelled for the man to let go of his daughter as he reached out trying to remove the man's hand but received a blow to the head with the butt of the gun. Dazed, he still had the ability to express the desire to take his daughter's place.

"Take me instead," he insisted.

"No you're about to be mayor. You're gonna be very useful to us. She's the perfect little motivation you'll need to do as you're told," the man informed Mason before finally snatching Bria out of her mother's arms as she cried out for Khari.

Khari screamed uncontrollably as she begged for the man to release her daughter to no avail as the door slammed shut and the men were gone along with Bria. Mason tried to console his distraught wife but she just kicked and screamed for him not to touch her, demanding him to bring back their daughter.

CHAPTER 19

"It's off, let's count it again," Kyrie said as he stood over the pile of money on the table with a blunt hanging from his mouth. "Y'all bitches better not be stashin'," he said looking down at the twins blowing out a cloud of smoke. Though he was young, Kyrie was straight business when it came to the drug game; the byproduct of being groomed by Sin from an early age. His no nonsense approach was the reason he had been entrusted with his own spot. Kyrie persuaded his boss to let him take over the spot on a slow block instead of shutting it down. He had it clicking in no time, turning it into one of the crew's most profitable spots. Sin was happy that the youngin' had convinced him to reconsider.

"Nigga you know better," said Cairo, the older of the twins by a few minutes. "Don't even play yaself," she said without looking up from counting.

"This nigga," Egypt said agreeing with her sister.

"I look like I'm playin'," he asked rhetorically. "We gon' count this shit again and we gonna keep countin' it until its right," Kyrie said as he took another hit of the weed before passing it to Cairo. His assertiveness turned her on, causing her to look up and smile at him before grabbing a stack of twenties and started to recount them.

Almost two hours had past when Kyrie placed the last stack of money inside the bag on the table. Zipping it up, he threw it over his shoulder before grabbing the second bag and throwing it over the other. "Aight I'm out," he said then headed out of the room. Entering the living room, he signaled to the two men waiting that he was ready, and they rose to their feet to follow him out to the car. With all the spots getting hit, Sin instructed everyone on his team to take added precautions when moving around and Kyrie had heeded the warning.

Looking up and down the block making sure everything was good, Kyrie began descending the steps when he felt the coast was clear. Hitting the sidewalk, closely guarded by the two armed men accompanying him, he pressed the button on his keys popping open his trunk. The light from inside the trunk cast a shadow on a man crouching down behind the car parked behind his.

"Yo it's a hit," Kyrie screamed just as the man popped up with a 12 gauge Mossberg in his hand.

The first shot hit the man to his left square in the chest

lifting him off his feet. Kyrie fell to the ground with him, dropping one of the bags while removing his gun from his waist. He quickly started returning fire along with the other guard with him. The man ducked back behind the car attempting to switch his position, giving Kyrie time to toss both bags over the gate landing behind the trash cans. He immediately heard shots hitting the gate behind him as another man popped up from behind a different car firing two Glock 9s. One of his shots struck the other guard in the shoulder causing him to drop his gun. The man holding the 12 gauge quickly reemerged and fired hitting him in the head dropping him instantly. Kyrie dove over the gate trying to take cover as the two men were now bearing down on him from opposite sides. He was out gunned and out manned. As the two men approached ready to finish off the youngster, the doors of the brownstone swung open and the twins popped out unloading bullets on the two men.

"Yeah niggas," Egypt screamed as she dumped her clip, swinging the odds back in Kyrie's favor, allowing him the rise to his feet and begin letting off again.

"Arrgh," one of the men screamed as two of Kyrie's bullets found their mark in his chest and stomach. "I'm hit," he yelled out to his partner as he felt the burning sensation shoot through his body.

His partner ducked behind a car trying to make his way over to his partner as bullets rained down on him, occasionally sending shots back. Finally, he made it over to him and seeing that he was in bad shape, he knew it was time to abort the mission. Dragging him behind the car he saw their getaway car speeding down the one way street in reverse and screech to a stop. He opened the back door pushing him in then getting in and yelling to the driver to pull off.

The twins raced down the steps to Kyrie.

"You okay baby?" Cairo asked checking to see if he was hit.

"Yeah I'm good," he replied. "Grab those bags, let's get the fuck outta here."

CHAPTER 20

Ashleigh circled the block a few times until she was able to find a parking spot, only a few houses away from her destination. She parked, quickly exited and hastily made her way up the block. She had been to see Case enough times that she felt comfortable driving herself to the unsavory neighborhood, but still kept her hand gripped around the taser in her coat pocket. Making her way up the block, she approached a crack head couple in the midst of an argument. They both paused at the sight of her, clearly noticing that she didn't belong to the neighborhood. Ashleigh gripped the taser tighter and her heartbeat sped up as her body filled with nervous energy. Her nervousness was laid to rest when the drug addicted woman flashed her rotten smile and complimented Ashleigh's beauty. She nodded and kept it moving up the block until she reached the bottom of Case's steps. Ascending them, she reached the door and noticed that it was slightly cracked, assuming he had left it that way anticipating her arrival she proceeded and entered. She was immediately greeted by what looked to be a trail of blood in the hallway leading to his door. The pace of her heartbeat quickened again as she slowly walked towards the door not knowing what she would see. Case's front door had a bloody hand print on it and was open just as the front door had been. Ashleigh called out his name but received no answer. She could faintly hear the sound of male voices coming from inside the apartment. Listening closely, she was able to decipher Case's voice and stepped inside and called his name.

Case paced the room back and forth, wrecking his brain trying to come up with a plan. He was short on time and needed to be quick about it. Focused on the task at hand he hadn't heard his name being called and turned aiming the 12 gauge in his hand when he heard Ashleigh enter the room.

"No," she screamed at the top of her lungs staring down the barrel of his gun.

Seeing her face, Case lowered his weapon to his side and began interrogating her. "What da fuck you doin' here?"

"We were supposed to get up tonight, remember?" she replied. "What's going on? Why is Dre bleeding?" she asked looking at his friend slumped on the couch. He looked to be in grave danger as blood poured from the wound in his stomach and he begged for help.

"I don't wanna die Case," Dre cried out.

"Nah, you good my nigga. You gonna be aight," he voiced giving his friend a false sense of hope because he, himself didn't believe that Dre was gonna make it.

"We have to get him to a hospital," Ashleigh stated vehemently.

"We can't, they gonna ask too many question," he informed her.

"Well what happened?" she quizzed.

"That shit ain't important right now Ash," he said growing frustrated with her. "Matter of fact you don't need to be here. You ain't built for this type of shit. Take ya bourgeois ass back to wherever the fuck you came from."

Ashleigh was taken aback by his bluntness because he had never spoken to her that way before. Her first thought was to storm out the door she had just came through, but feeling the need to prove herself and earn some street cred in his eyes, she came up with an idea. Pulling out her phone she scrolled down her call log and pressed send.

"What are you doing?" Case asked. "Who the fuck are you calling?" he said attempting to take the phone from her.

"Somebody that can help," she informed.

* * *

Ashleigh peaked her head out the front door, seeing the black SUV pulling up she called out to Case. He emerged from the apartment with Dre's arm around his neck as he helped him to the door and down the steps to the waiting vehicle. After getting his friend into the truck Case hopped in. Ashleigh introduced him to her driver Rick, whom she had called knowing he wouldn't mention the situation to her father but also because he knew the doctor her father used to take care of things like this without involving hospitals or the police.

Case was impressed by Ashleigh. He had clearly misjudged her, assuming her to be a trust fund kid, whose parents were too busy to care what she was up to, so they spoiled her with luxuries to keep her happy. Though he was partially right, there was much more to her than met the eyes. He was now admittedly intrigued by the connections she might have after seeing her make the type of call she had. Who da fuck is this bitch and what type of shit she got going on, he thought to himself while still trying to keep Dre's spirits up. "We almost there my nigga, just hold on," he encouraged.

"I'm not gonna make it my nigga. I'm dying," Dre moaned.

"Nah you good, just hold on," he insisted but he knew his friend's chances were fading fast.

Dre sounded like a wounded animal as his moans increased. "I don't wanna die Case," Dre cried.

"How much longer?" Case asked looking up at the driver, the look on his face was one of hopelessness. He and Dre had been friends all their life; their mothers had been best friends since their teenaged years. Both women had gotten pregnant at sixteen and vowed that their sons would be as tight as they were. They were brothers from another mother in every sense of the phrase.

The SUV pulled into the driveway of a craftsman style home in Belleville, New Jersey and pulled into the opened garage. As the door closed Case saw a small Jewish man standing in the doorway.

"That's the doc right there," the driver informed them.

Case, excited to finally arrive, couldn't wait to get his friend medical attention. "C'mon Dre we're here," he said looking over at his friend who laid lifeless against the door of the truck unresponsive. "Dre! Dre!" Case screamed as he shook him trying to awake him. "Nooo! C'mon Dre say something!" he pleaded but it was already too late.

"He's gone," the driver said as he watched the young man lean back in his seat fighting back tears. "I don't know what kind of shit you into young man, but it's obvious you're in deep. So as a favor to Ms. Ashleigh here, I'm gonna offer you a life line. I can tell ol' boy was ya man but you don't need him popping up on no slabs in the morgue. That's gonna bring all types of attention you obviously don't need."

"What you getting at my man?" Case asked wishing to skip the long speeches.

"The Doc can perform his magic and this body will disappear," the driver revealed.

Case didn't want to do his man like that but he knew if people connected the dots from the shootout and Dre's death, it wouldn't be long before there was a price on his head and the police were beating down his door. After he thought about it for a moment the choice really was a no brainer.

CHAPTER 21

Ariane was awakened by the sound of Sin's phone ringing on the nightstand next to him. The sound seemed deafening to her, but he laid there sound asleep. *How he don't hear that shit,* she thought to herself, as the phone started to ring once again. "Sin," she said shaking him. After several attempts he sat up in the bed finally hearing it for himself. The light from his phone illuminated the darkened room making it easy to locate on the nightstand. Picking it up, he saw his sister Cassie's name flashing across the screen and quickly answered knowing that if she was trying to reach him this late it had to be important.

"What's wrong Cass?" he asked.

Cassie answered quickly without preamble. "It's dad, he's been shot...."

* * *

The streets of New York seemed to pass in a blur as Sin raced through the city with Ariane in route to the hospital in Manhattan. Entering the doors of the lobby, he made a beeline for the front desk then jumped on the elevator after receiving the floor his father had been taken to. As the elevator doors opened, Sin and Ariane stepped out into the waiting room and were greeted by wet eyes and the worried filled faces of the Holloway clan. Mason tossed idle threats in the air while pacing back and forth in the middle of the room as his grief stricken wife sat inconsolable in a chair not too far from him. Emma sat in a corner clutching a Bible with Jewlz at her side rubbing her back. Never had he seen her look less than flawless, but her running massacre and disheveled appearance was anything but. Cassie rose from her seat next to her husband to greet Sin. He could tell she had been crying but was doing her best to keep it together.

"What's up?" Sin asked anxiously awaiting word on his father.

"Uncle Nate is dead and Daddy is still in surgery," Cassie relayed as she fought back tears, then fell into her brother's arms, burying her head in his chest and bawling like a child. "And they took Bria," she cried out.

Sin's eyes shifted to Khari, desolated by the kidnapping of her daughter, her lack of emotional stability now made perfect sense.

Ariane remained silent only placing a hand on his back for comfort. Her mind flooded with questions, realizing she hadn't asked Sin much about his family. Now she was standing amongst them in the midst of a crisis looking like a deer in headlights. This surely wasn't how she planned on meeting them. Scanning the room she immediately recognized Mason as the candidate from the campaign commercials all over TV. His presence only added to her questions. Is that his brother? she thought.

Sin, noticing the look of confusion painted on her face, released his sister from his embrace and introduced the two women. "This is my sister Cassie," he said. "Cassie this is..."

"Ariane," she said surprising the woman by knowing who she was. "Hi, it's nice to finally meet you."

"Nice to meet you too," Ariane said still a little shocked. It was obvious Sin had mentioned her to his sister, which was a good thing in her eyes.

Jewlz stood up and crossed the room to hug his brother to his mother's dismay. Even the current state of events couldn't thaw her frigid feelings towards him. She stared at him wishing he had not shown his face. He was the cancer she couldn't get rid of. Overcome by grief and anger she lashed out at him and Mason followed suit.

"Why are you here?" Emma sneered at Sin. "What, you have your little thugs outside waiting for you? What they going to do? What the hell you are going to do? Nothing! My husband puts so much interest and trust into you. For what? Where were you when the bullets were piercing his body? Too busy running around like you some big tough guy but you're no good to anyone when it counts, you ain't shit and you never will be just like your raggedy ass excuse of a mother."

Usually whatever Emma would have to say to Sin wouldn't bother him. He would never show any emotion. He always brushed her snide remarks off or just smiled at her knowing that would eat at her skin even more, but with the possibly fatal assassination attempt on his father and the disrespect towards his late mother he decided at this point he had to give her a taste of her own disrespect.

"You even had the nerve to drag some trash in here with you," Emma stated and darted her eyes towards Ariane.

"Why don't you shut the fuck up for once! You keep running that hole in your face like you run something or someone. You might run the rest of these muthafuckas, but you never could run me or my father. As for my mother on her worst day you would've never amounted to the woman she was, ask your husband! Now I would appreciate it if you stepped the fuck out my way so I can check on my Pops!" Sin's words pierced through Emma's soul. It took everything in her to not slap him across his face.

Before Emma could say anything Mason jumped in the way to his mother's defense immediately. "Get your friend and leave now. Our family doesn't need your bullshit right now and I won't tolerate you disrespecting my mother in anyway. Nobody gives a fuck about you but Pops and he ain't able to jump to your defense right now so just leave."

Sin flared his nose and stood eye to eye with his older half -brother with his index finger pointed in his face. "Yo, my nigga you got half a second to get up out my face with that rah rah shit before I show your moms how much of a bitch you are."

Ariane tugged at Sin's arm trying to get him to avoid the situation about to happen, but he pulled away from her and pushed her to the side. As soon as Mason stepped closer to Sin to reply he hit him with a two piece, dropping him in the middle of the waiting room.

Emma lunged at him only to be intercepted. "Ma," Cassie screamed getting between the two of them. "What is your problem? Sin has just as much right to be here as anybody. Regardless of how you may feel he is our brother...all of us," she said looking at Mason. "And at a time like this family is more important than anything. Daddy would want him here, so cut the shit Ma."

Emma cut her eyes at her daughter. It hadn't been the first time Cassie had taken a stand against her. Out of all her children she was the one who feared her mother the least and valued her opinion even less. They had notoriously bumped heads since Cassie's rebellious teenage years. Cassie never fell under her mother's wing the way Ashleigh had. Never one for the country club high society scene, she had always respected the hustle and boss status of her father more than the bourgeois ways of her mother. "Cassie you're an idiot just like your father, don't you ever jump to anyone's defense who is not a Holloway!" Emma yelled at her daughter.

"Mom get over yourself! It's not a Holloway thing, it's a you thing. It's always been, can you stop being self-absorbed for once in your life and focus on what's important here. Daddy is in there fighting for his life and all you can worry about is who is welcome at your table and who is not! I'm tired of you and your antics," Cassie was embarrassed and ashamed of her mother's behavior.

The doors of the operating room swung open and the doctor entered with a blank stare, making the news he was about to deliver undetectable. There was an eerie silence in the room as he plodded towards them seemingly in slow motion. All eyes in the room were now on him. Emma stood directly in front of him, clutching her bible close to her chest as she braced for the news.

"Mr. Holloway suffered multiple gunshot wounds as a result of his attack; one in his hand, another in his upper arm which fractured his shoulder. And I had to remove a bullet that was lodged in his back. He is out of surgery and I expect him to make a full recovery," the doctor explained.

"So can we see him now?" Emma asked.

"I don't see why not," he replied.

Sin entered the room last, the sight of his father in the hospital bed with bandages over his wounds had a fire burning in the pit of his stomach. But in true Sin fashion his exterior remained emotionless. It was one of his strongest attributes; it made him hard to read to friends and enemies alike. Taking his place at the foot of the bed, while Emma and the rest of his siblings stood by his bedside, he stared at his father who slowly opened his eyes at the sound of all the people in the room.

Marion was in a considerable amount of pain as the medicine had begun to wear off some. His right arm was in a sling from his shoulder being shattered by a bullet. Forced to take short breaths, his back felt as though he had been hit by a sledgehammer and hurt every time he inhaled or exhaled. He sat propped up in the bed as the family took turns asking him questions. His mood remained somber as he noticed how every avoided telling him how his longtime friend Nate was doing. He could see the looks in their eyes when he asked the question and immediately knew that he hadn't been as lucky. Finally, Sin spoke up confirming what he already knew.

"I'm sorry Pops. Uncle Nate is dead."

"And they took Bria," Mason cried out.

The news hurt more than any bullet. All his life he had went out of his way to protect his family and keep them out of harm's way and hearing that his granddaughter had somehow been caught up in his criminal web shook him to his core. He closed his eyes and bit down on his lips in order to hold back the tears he felt forming in the wells of his eyes.

"Clear the room," Marion grunted. "Except you," he continued nodding towards Sin. Mason, much to his chagrin, wasn't asked to stay.

The sound of the machines beeping seemed to grow louder as the room door closed leaving the two men alone. Sin pulled a chair up to the side of the bed and sat next to his father. "Di Toro?" he asked not needing to say much else for his father to understand the question.

Marion just nodded, he had played his hand wrong, something he rarely did and it had cost his family greatly. "You were right son," he admitted. "I should have listened to you. We should have moved on Di Toro and his family a long time ago."

Sin claimed no victory in being right. The level of respect and admiration he held for his father was too great to do such a thing. His only concern at the moment was retribution. He wouldn't rest until he had exacted revenge and wiped out Mike Di Toro and the entire Martello family. They had drawn first blood but he planned to paint the town red with theirs.

His thoughts were interrupted by the door being opened. Federal Agent Mosley entered the room with a contemptuous look sprawled across his face. "Marion Holloway," he said.

"Roosevelt Mosley," Marion replied. "Longtime no see. What do I owe the pleasure?"

"Just stopped in to see how you were doing," Mosley stated.

"I've been better," Marion grunted. "But you know that right. You're the government, you know everything," he cracked.

"You know what I know?" he rhetorically questioned. "Mike Di Toro is trying to put you out of business and from where I'm standing it looks like he's doing a pretty good job."

"I don't know what you're talking about. I run nothing but legitimate businesses," Marion informed him.

"I know he doesn't," the agent said pointing to Sin who just stared at him with a menacing look. "Omerta," he laughed. "Didn't think that applied to the niggas," he teased.

"Once Di Toro finds out you're not dead, he's going to come after you even harder. You just better pray he gets to you before I do because mine will be a slow and painful death behind concrete and steel."

Marion smirked as Mosley exited the room. They had history. The squabble between the two dated back decades. Mosley had a personal vendetta, the root of which still remained a mystery to him. Marion was used to the feds lurking so him showing up to the hospital wasn't a surprise.

"Fucking feds," Sin said in disgust.

"It's to be expected. With all the bodies dropping it was only a matter of time," Marion schooled his son.

"Yeah, I know. But he is right about one thing," Sin confessed. "Once word gets out that you're not dead, you won't be safe here. We need to move you to the house."

Marion nodded in agreement.

* * *

Ariane stood in the mirror of the hospital bathroom trying to wrap her mind around what she had walked into. The man she was in love with had a brother that was running for mayor, an evil stepmother and a father laid up in the hospital filled with bullet holes for God knows what reason. It all seemed like a movie to her. She washed her hands and walked out the door.

Sin stepped into the hallway from his father's room just in time to see her walking down the hallway to where the family had gathered outside the room. Sin grabbed her hand and held it in his, kissing it gently and asked if she was ok.

"I should be asking you that."

"I'm good cuz you here," he stated before turning his attention to the family. "Listen y'all, we need to get Pops outta here tonight!" he said.

"Out of where?" Mason questioned with his lip slightly swollen from his altercation with Sin. "The hospital?"

"Yeah, we don't know why this happened or who's responsible for it and for all we know they could come in here and finish Pops off in the middle of the night."

"That's why we have guards. I want them downstairs in the lobby and in front of this door 24/7." Mason ordered trying to show some sort of authority.

"The hospital will not allow Pops to have his own personal armed security, unless you can pull some of those political strings you got," Sin paused waiting for his answer but none came. "I didn't think so, like I said we gotta get Pops to the house. I've spoken with him about it already, so it's nothing more to talk about."

Mason looked at this mother waiting for her to object and side with him but to his great surprise she cosigned Sin's proposal. "As much as I hate to admit it," she began. "He's absolutely right. Your father is not safe here. And until we know who is behind this, the best place for him is at home."

CHAPTER 22

The uneasiness could be felt as soon as the caravan of vehicles entered through the gate of the Holloway Estate behind the private ambulance that was carrying the leader of their family. Ariane stared in amazement at the sight of the elaborate home, but more at the mob of armed men patrolling the grounds. It was as if they had their own secret service. She tried to take it all in, but it only added to her questions and heightened her confusion. But she understood now wasn't the time to ask questions. Sin was dealing with a lot and she didn't want to complicate things any more than they already were. As the ambulance came to a stop in front of the house, members of the security team assisted the medics removing Marion and getting him up to his bedroom so he could rest comfortably. Sin leaned against a wall in the living room with his phone to his ear as the rest of the family sat around the TV looking distraught as they watched the reports on the news. Khari, no longer able to watch after seeing the picture of Bria flash across the screen, had to be sedated in order to soothe her emotions. Mason escorted her upstairs so she could rest before quickly returning and joining the group.

Emma descended the steps a few minutes after him, returning from checking on her husband. Her mind on the one missing face. "Has anybody been able to reach Ashleigh yet?"

"No Ma, I've been calling her for the past hour, still nothing." Jewlz informed her.

"This is too much," Emma replied as she sat in an empty chair shaking her head in frustration.

The bell ringing caught the attention of everyone in the room as none of them was expecting any visitors; no one except Sin who knew exactly who it was. Beans bopped into the living room accompanied by Sheik, Barkim and Ali. It was the first time they had ever been to the Holloway Estate but Sin needed the people he trusted the most around him. He knew Di Toro was behind the hit on his father but wasn't sure if someone in Marion's organization had assisted in setting his father up and he couldn't afford to take the chance. He greeted the men and they excused themselves into another room to speak.

"Yo, them niggas hit another one of our spots tonight," Beans said to his surprise.

"Fuck!"

"Them niggas, ain't get shit tho," Beans continued.

"Youngin and the twins backed them niggas down," Sheik said proudly. "Boy said he hit one of em' up."

"Get the word to our people. See who has shown up to the hospitals tonight with a gunshot wound."

"Already on it," Sheik relayed. "I shut the spot down myself, so it ain't shit to worry about with that either."

"Yeah and I got them laying up in one of our low spots 'til this shit blow over." Beans explained.

"Good job, but I need us at full strength right now. These muthafuckas hit my Pops up, killed my uncle and kidnapped my niece. We gotta move on these niggas ASAP. That shit with the spots can wait, won't be no spots if this nigga Di Toro takeover. I don't trust none of these muthafuckas my Pops got wit him, that's why y'all here. Get on the horn and get everybody here. And tell youngin to bring those twins wit em."

Sin stepped back into the living room to check on Ariane, who sat on a chaise lounge looking out of place. Always very observant, she was slowly beginning to realize that Marion was a lot more important than just the next mayor's father. After all what sense does it make to try to assassinate a candidate's father, she thought to herself. She also noticed how the secret service looking men kept reporting back to Sin and not Mason and every conversation he was having seemed to be done in a whisper or with him stepping into another room. She felt so out of place and all the secret talks weren't helping.

"You ok?" he asked sitting down next to her. "You need anything?"

"I'm ok, just feeling a lil' out of place. I don't really belong here...now, at this time, with everything going on. I see you keep having to go in another room to talk or whisper. I don't mean to intrude. I feel like y'all can't be regular because I'm here."

"First off, you belong anywhere I'm at. And for two, this is the norm around here," he said looking around. "My father is a very important man, who means a lot to a lot people. That's why it's so hectic right now." Sin stroked the side of her face causing her to look up at him. His eyes showed he was attentive to her feelings and had every intention on explaining everything to her.

Everything in her knew who Sin was. She had always known but tried ignoring the signs. Fact was Ariane didn't want to know the truth. It would shatter the fairy tale she had created in her mind. But this was one level of things she had never seen before and it made her nervous.

* * *

Ashleigh dropped the tissue into the toilet and flushed it. Standing up and pulling up her panties she cut off the light and exited the bathroom into the dimly lit bedroom. Case laid in the bed snoring lightly as she tip-toed around the bed over to the dresser not wanting to wake him. Picking her phone off the dresser, she touched the screen but nothing happen. She realized that it was dead and for how long she had no idea. Retrieving her charger from her bag she plugged it in and as soon as it came on the messages started to make it vibrate in her hand. Quietly checking her voicemail she heard the voice of her younger brother Jewlz, saying that she needed to come home as soon as she received his message. Assuming it to be nothing more than her parents trying to find out where she was and what she was up to, she dialed his number back to see what was going on.

"Hello," she said nonchalantly.

"Ashleigh where the hell are you? I been calling your phone for hours," Jewlz stated. "You need to get to the house now. Pops got shot, Uncle Nate is dead and Bria is missing..."

Ashleigh dropped the phone, screaming as tears raced down her face one after the other. Her loud cry woke Case from his slumber. He jumped up in the bed and turned on the lamp on the nightstand.

"What's wrong!" he shouted seeing her hysterically crying.

"My father!" she cried. "They shot my father..."

"What?" he said jumping out the bed, racing over to her and holding her in his arms. "What happened?"

"I don't know. I just know my father got shot, my uncle

is dead and my niece is missing."

Case walked her over to the bed sitting her down. Only hours earlier he had lost his best friend and she had been there for him, now it was his turn. "It's gonna be alright," he said as he held her and rubbed her gently on her head.

"Oh my God, why is this happening?" she sobbed while resting her head in his chest. "My brother is gonna kill whoever is responsible for this," she said in anger. "I know he is." She got up from his embrace and began pacing the room looking for and grabbing her things.

Her claim caught Case by surprise as he had never heard her speak about her siblings or her family period. So for her to make a statement with such bravado shocked him. But after seeing the type of connections she showed earlier in the night, helping him handle Dre's shooting, he was interested in knowing more. With Dre dead, he would definitely need a new hustle. He figured if he played his cards right with Ashleigh he could find himself a whole new means of getting bread. "Your brother?" he inquired while standing up from the bed and walking over to her by the mirror as she threw a sloppy ponytail in her head.

"Yeah, my brother Sin," she bragged, turning around now and facing him. "He runs shit, and he gonna body whoever did this to my family." She walked over to the bed and grabbed her shoes that sat beside it.

Hearing the name made his face change. Sin, he thought

to himself, can't be. He could not believe what he was hearing. "Run shit where?" he asked.

"All over but definitely out in Brooklyn," she revealed. "You ever heard of him?"

"Not that I can remember," he said, pretending while trying to soak up information. What were the chances of the chick he had been smashing all these months being the sister of the nigga whose spots he had been robbing. His blood began to boil at the thought of being able to put a slug in Sin's head and any member of his crew as payback for Dre. *I can't let that ride. I'ma kill that nigga and every nigga that roll wit' em. Worse come to worst I'll just body this bitch and send her to him in pieces,* he thought, continuing to watch Ashleigh scramble around the room looking for her things.

Ashleigh walked back and forth a couple times seemingly unable to grab hold of her thoughts. Case seeing her move around frantically as her hands trembled noticeably, took the opportunity to put his plan in motion.

"Let me help you," he said gathering her things for her. "You're in no shape to be driving. Hold on for a second and let me get my sneakers. I'll take you home."

"What about my car?"

"Have your driver bring you to get it whenever you ready. It's safe with me," he assured her, adding a smile for the finishing touches. She felt good to have Case by her side at that very moment. Earlier that night he was the one who was going through some bullshit with Dre and she was able to come through for him. Now he was reciprocating it back to her with the turmoil that just landed on her family. At the very moment his support and embrace made her feel good and safe. Which made it easier for her to open up to him. She had someone on her side to hold her down that wasn't ordered or hired by her father or her brother. He was her nigga and she liked the feeling.

* * *

Sin sat at the head of the table in the seat that was usually reserved for his father. Seeing him there represented a change of the guard. Though temporary, it gave everyone in the room a glimpse into the future. Beans sat directly to his right, occupying Uncle Nate's old chair. He had always been Sin's second in command and that wouldn't change now. Sin's eyes scanned the room at the familiar faces he now sat amongst, his crew along with members of his father's crew. Though the two men heavily resembled each other, they had two different styles when it came to conducting business, something the holdovers from Marion's regime was about to find out.

"I'ma keep this short and sweet. Anybody in this room not prepared to go to war, right now is your opportunity to leave. There's the door," he said before pausing.

None of the other men spoke. All of them were good listeners and very patient men. They had one other thing in common; they were men who had refused to conform to the rules of society. There was no force or mortal man who could bend them to his will unless they wished it. They were men who guarded their free will with artfulness and murder and could only be undermined by death or extreme reasoning. Sin would not need to resort to any of that, every man who sat across from him was of one mind and one mission.

"Ok then, we gonna hit Di Toro and his peoples and we gonna hit em hard." Nothing more needed to be said. The room remained silent leaving Sin's words the last spoken. Everyone knew what it was and was ready.

* * *

Emma strutted towards Ariane holding a bottle of wine and two glasses in her hand. Stopping right in front of her she placed the glasses down on the table. "Chardonnay?"

Ariane, in need of a stiff drink, wished she had offered something stronger but she wasn't going to turn it down. She was still unsure of how she felt about the Holloway matriarch after her not so friendly words at the hospital. But she nodded her head accepting the offer.

"First, let me apologize for my behavior at the hospital earlier. I was upset and I took it out on Sin and you caught some of the shrapnel. I meant neither of you any harm my dear, just had a lot of emotions going on."

Ariane remained skeptical of the woman. She had seen

her fangs at the hospital and wasn't so sure if her act of contrition was just that, an act. Taking a sip from her freshly filled glass, she only offered a thank you for the wine.

"So how long have you and Yasin been dating?"

"A few months."

"That's good. I remember when his father and I first started dating. Those two have a lot of the same ways, so I can relate to that look you have in your eyes when you stare at him. It's something about the men in this family. But definitely those two."

"He hasn't spoken much about his family."

"Really?" Emma asked seeing an opportunity to stir up something. "That's interesting. He did tell you what it is that he does for a living hasn't he, or has he kept that a secret as well?" Emma made eye contact with Ariane and displayed a devilish smirk as she knew how she would play her hand; let Ariane fall into her line of questioning.

"No I know he sells cars. We actually met at the dealership."

"Oh no, that's just a front my dear," Emma slyly said. "Sin is a drug dealer darling. He sells drugs and kills people for a living," she bluntly stated. She knew she had hit a nerve from the look on the young woman's face so she continued. "I'm just telling you so you won't be in the dark while dealing with him. Like right now he and his group of thugs are upstairs plotting on payback for whoever did this to my husband. I would prefer to get the police involved but you saw his temper at the hospital, I wouldn't dare challenge him. Oh, and please don't you try challenging him either. My advice to you is to walk while you have a chance, don't get in too deep honey. Men like him will never give up their lifestyle for a woman. You either adapt or you leave. But if you stick around then think you gonna make a break for it," she pause letting her voice tail off. "Sweetheart you become a liability and men in this business don't keep those around. All loose ends get tied up."

Ariane's stomach sunk deep with each word Emma spilled out of her mouth. Her hands got clammy and her mouth became dry. She couldn't believe what the woman in front of her was telling her about the man she loved.

Just then Sin came around the corner. Seeing the look on Ariane's face and Emma sitting next to her he knew something was wrong.

"Excuse me," Ariane said placing her glass on the table, popping up from her seat and stalking towards him. "I wanna go home."

Her look was one he hadn't seen from her. Her lips were clinched tight and her eyes were piercing as she stomped out the front door of the house with him on her heels. "What's wrong wit you?" he asked. "What did that evil woman say to you?"

"Sin I'm gonna ask you this one time and don't lie to me.

What do you do for a living?"

Hearing the question, he already knew what Emma was discussing with her. "I sell cars Ariane."

"Don't lie to me!" she shouted.

"I sell cars Ariane," he said refusing to look her in her face, knowing that she wanted no parts of the life he was heavily involved in. Even if she was able to deal with it, the depth of his involvement would probably be too much for her to bear. Here he was, standing on the verge of losing another woman he loved due to his ties to the streets. Ariane, however, was different. She was actually used to the life and was built for the role of the wife of a street king; she just wanted no parts of the game after losing her brother. And she had made that crystal clear to him.

"At least be a man about it Sin and tell me the truth," she pleaded needing to hear him say the words that she knew in her heart were true.

He turned his head and looked her in her eyes and said, "I sell cars."

Her heart cracked. She felt like the wind had been knocked out of her. She loved the man standing in front of her so much and couldn't believe he wouldn't admit what they both know. Heartbreak turned to anger as she reached back to slap him but he caught her hand and tried pulling her into him for a hug.

"Just come back inside. We can talk about all this later."

"I wanna go home. Get me out of here," she said unable to be swayed by him as tears rolled down her face.

CHAPTER 23

"It's coming up on the right," Ashleigh pointed directing Case as they rode through the affluent neighborhood in Westchester.

He remained silent but was mesmerized by the lavish homes they passed in route. Pulling up to the gate Case couldn't contain himself any longer. "You live here?"

"This my parent's house. I stay here from time to time. But I own a condo in Manhattan," she informed him.

As the gate opened Case got a full view of the massive estate tucked behind the giant wall and large trees. Ashleigh's people were rich and that meant to him that Sin was actually getting more money than he had originally thought. Damn this bitch is connected, he thought, pulling into the large parking area in front of the home. He watched as Sin escorted a thick, shapely beauty across the driveway into a waiting dark tinted vehicle and watched as it pulled through the gate and disappeared. Seeing him standing alone, Case had the urge to remove the gun tucked in his waist, jump out and put a couple rounds in him. But he decided to play it cool, knowing he had no chance of making it out alive due to all the armed men positioned throughout the property. His pulse quickened, filling him with rage as the front door opened and Kyrie emerged from the house joining Sin in the driveway. Putting the car in park and placing his hand on his gun he fixed his eyes on the two men engaged in a conversation. Noticing Ashleigh exiting the car they turned and walked towards her.

"You not gonna get out?" she asked looking back into the car.

"Nah ma, I just wanted to make sure you got here safe. I need to get back to the city. You got me out here in the boonies," he said with a joking smile.

"Ok thank you, I call you later."

"No doubt."

Ashleigh closed the door and watched him pull off and through the gate just as her brother and Kyrie walked up on her.

"Where the fuck you been?" Sin asked still in a bad mood from his argument with Ariane but also pissed at not being able to reach her for hours. "And who was that?"

"You not my father Sin, so I don't know who you think you talking to," she snapped.

"What! These muthafuckas tried to kill your father

tonight, murked Uncle Nate and snatched Bria. You out here parading around like Miss America. The Italians don't give a fuck bout none of that. They'll cut ya pretty lil' head off and send it to ya moms in there."

Ashleigh just lowered her head understanding the seriousness in his tone. "Is Daddy ok? How's Khari doing?" her attitude now gone as she spoke.

"Go in there and see for yourself." Sin watched her disappear into the house then turned continuing his talk with Kyrie. "I heard the twins handled themselves real well out there tonight."

"Yea, I told you, I got them trained to go. Them bitches will murk anybody I say," Kyrie bragged.

"I got a job for y'all then. We need to get at these Italians. You ready for that?" Sin asked looking him in the eyes searching for any traces of doubt in the young gunner. "This a whole notha level."

"Murder is murder, just tell me what you need me to do."

* * *

Mason sat in his parents' den alone working on his second glass of cognac; the upcoming election the furthest thing from his mind. He kept replaying the sequence of events that led to his daughter being kidnapped. Uncle Nate was gone and his father would heal but the uncertainty surrounding Bria was killing him. *What did they mean by she was the proper motivation I would need to do as I was told? What did they want?* Those questions and more danced around in his head as he sat staring at the bottom of his glass again. He twisted the top off the crystal liquor decanter and poured himself another drink.

"So you just gonna sit there drinking while our daughter is out there somewhere, with God knows what happening to her," Khari said as she stood in the door glaring at him. "Some leader you are. No wonder why you're trailing in the election."

"What, you ran out of pills to pop?" he countered before sipping his drink. In no way was he in the mood to deal with her and her bullshit. "You've got some nerve. You're a borderline junkie."

"Fuck you," she said with tears streaming down her face.

"No fuck you," he snapped. "Look at you, no matter how much make up you put on or how many designer labels you dress in, under it all you're still just a hood rat from Fort Greene. I'm glad Bria has a woman like my mother around to look up to."

"Your mother, please! She a conniving, manipulating bitch. That's who you want your daughter to grow up and be? Give me a fucking break I'll roll over twice in my grave before I let my daughter turn out like her"

"Better that than a washed up...good for nothing...wannabe actress slash junkie," he said rising to his feet. "I'm gonna get my daughter back. You just hope you're not the next one to go missing. Stupid bitch," he said now only a few inches from her face. "I made you. Remember that without me you would be nothing."

The smell of alcohol filled her nostrils. She had seen this movie before and knew better than to say something back. Fighting back tears she lowered her head, not wanting to give him anymore satisfaction. Mason bumped his shoulder into her on his way out the door. Khari walked over to the couch as the tears began to trickle down her face. She had gotten herself in over her head with Mason. She kept up a happy exterior for the cameras and everyone on the outside but she was so unhappy that she had even contemplated taking her own life. The only thing stopping her was the thought of leaving her kids to be raised by Mason and Emma. If they had their way her kids wouldn't even remember her. She grabbed the open bottle of liquor and took a swig. The burn in her chest almost made her throw up, but she ignored it and took another one than collapsed on the couch in tears.

Sin could hear the slight whimpers coming from the den so he walked to the door and peeked in. Seeing Khari, his first thought was to keep it moving, acting as though he didn't see or hear a thing. But no matter how much disdain he held towards her, he truly felt sorry for her with Bria missing. He knew how much she cared for her children and could see she was in a lot of pain. Still he turned to walk away only to be stopped by her calling his name.

"I see you standing there," she said. "You're probably

taking some sort of pleasure in all of this huh?"

"You know better, that ain't never been my thing," he answered stepping in the room.

"Who are you kidding Sin? I know you hate me. You haven't spoken a word to me in years."

"Nah I don't hate you Khari. I did once but that was a longtime ago. You made your choice, you did what you felt was best for you. Now you have to live that life you chose."

"I never meant to hurt you," she tried explaining only to be cut off.

"That's not even important anymore."

"But I needed to say it, even if it was just for my own personal reasons. I did what I thought was best at the time."

The two of them shared an awkward history. They had grown up in the same slums of Fort Greene Projects. Khari however wasn't your ordinary project chick. She hated living in subsidized housing, so she made it her mission as a young teenage girl to bust her ass in school, taking day and night classes along with summer school to graduate early. She despised the fact that both her parents worked two jobs and barely managed to take care of her and her two younger sisters; struggling to make them comfortable in their cramped up two bedroom apartment. She promised herself that wouldn't be her life forever and the first chance she had to get out she would.

Khari was smart and beautiful, standing 5'6 and weighing

130 pounds that had been distributed in all the proper places. Her cocoa brown complexion glowed when the sun hit it. She kept her long black hair layered and her brown eyes accentuated her beauty, melting hearts with a single look. Her stomach was flat, despite giving birth twice, and made her breast appear larger than they were. What wasn't an illusion was her nice round ass which provided all the curves the slim built beauty needed. Her voice was soft and when she spoke you could hear the slight accent that remained from being raised by Jamaican parents.

* * *

As a young girl in the projects she never liked to draw attention to herself, only wearing baggy jeans and big t-shirts in hopes of going undetected by the boys in her school and the hustlers in front of her building. She knew that the right pair of jeans could attract the wrong type of nigga. Nothing or no one peaked her interest besides school and thoughts of earning a scholarship. So having many friends or a boyfriend for that matter was not an option. But that all changed one day when she got off her train after school and stopped at the corner bodega to get a beef patty with cocoa bread.

Sin stood at the counter waiting to place his order for a sandwich, wearing a black North Face jacket, some jeans and a pair of timberland boots. "You can go before me shorty," he said.

"I'on know what I want yet," lying, knowing he ordered the same thing every day but he had to say something to her. He

had watched her for weeks come and go from her building to the train station. He noticed how she was always alone. Never running with a crowd of females or any of the local niggas. He admired how she always seemed to be in her own world, like she didn't belong amongst the rats, the roaches and poverty stricken people of the desolate projects. He could see the determination in her eyes to get out, sort of how he moved and felt.

Sin was a young hustler. Wise beyond his years and in search of something bigger. Bigger than just being a corner boy, a hand to hand block hustler working off the next niggas pack. That wasn't for him, he was determined to find a come up. He had plans on one day owning the very blocks he hustled on. Not only as the top guy supplying the streets but actually owning the buildings on the block, real estate. It was that type of thinking that separated him from the guys his age and placed him head and shoulders above the group of hoodlums he ran with. It wouldn't be long before he was a well-respected leader of his own crew of young hustlers.

"Are you sure?" Khari replied now trying to hide the fact that she was blushing, by putting her head down. She hadn't expected the bronze skinned baby face to be so handsome when he turned around. It was too late he noticed it and smiled.

"Yeah, it's cool. Today must be your lucky day," Sin playfully teased.

"Lucky huh?" Khari asked.

"Yea ... Lucky," Sin reiterated.

"Three seventy five," the Puerto Rican man behind the

counter shouted to Khari.

"I got it Papi," replied Sin, never losing eye contact with her.

"No I'm good. I got my own money," she insisted.

"I'm sure you do and I mean no disrespect but I want to buy it. It's the least you could do for cutting me in line," Sin stated jokingly.

"So you want to pay for my food because you let me cut you in line?"

"Yup and I want to walk you to your building too. Ya know, make sure you get there safe. Can't have you getting robbed for that food I just bought, niggas is crazy out here. Plus I don't like wasting money," he said causing her to laugh.

"Oh you're hilarious..." Khari said pausing realizing she didn't catch his name.

"Yasin," he said smoothly.

"Okay Yasin," she said letting his name roll off her tongue sweetly.

"So you not gonna tell me your name?" Sin asked.

"It depends," she quickly answered.

"On what?"

"If I'm still smiling by the time you finish walking me to my building," Khari said grabbing her food and walking out of the bodega.

Khari was intrigued by him and Sin was by her. He was engaging. His conversation was not at all what she expected for a guy who sold drugs. He wanted to know more about her as well *and planned on using all his charm to get her to let him into her life. Eventually it worked and the two of them became inseparable. She was the missing piece to his puzzle and there was nothing that he would not do for her. Her days of riding the subways to school alone were over. He would wait for her in the morning to ride with her and be there at night to pick her up. Every plan in his life now involved Khari, which made him hustle harder and more diligently. Her dreams of becoming an actress were almost shattered after getting accepted into the Tisch School of Arts at NYU and her parents couldn't afford the partial tuition. Sin refused to let her dream die. Wanting to see it happen for her, he paid the tab allowing her to chase her dreams. As he climbed up the ladder in the street, he spoiled her more; buying her jewelry and keeping her draped in all the latest fashions. He encouraged her to embrace her beauty and taught her to love her curvaceous body; making love to it, opening her mind up and allowing her body to experience feelings she never dreamed imaginable. She had touched herself before but had never been able to orgasm until Sin went down on her and sent her into nirvana. The once innocent little girl became a woman under his sexual tutelage.*

"You are my woman, you deserve the best, and the world should always see you at your best." He would always tell her. Sin tried his best to convince her to move in with him, but she would always refuse; her excuse of wanting to get the full experience of college life, which included living in the dorms. It always seemed legit to him but was only half true. Khari knew how her education

was afforded and how she was able to sport every expensive label out at the time. She was fully aware of his occupation. But she also knew fast money didn't last and she longed for something more stable. She never wanted to be a hustler's girl to begin with, but those were the cards that life had dealt her at the time so she played them. She loved Sin without a doubt, but she was terrified of the life he lived and it had only seemed to become more dangerous the bigger he became in the streets. She missed the days when they went anywhere they wanted without a care in the world. They still did but people reacted to him differently now. For his part Sin never changed one bit, his main concern remained her. Females would do anything to garner his attention but he remained loyal to Khari only trying to make a better life for the two of them the best way he knew how.

Their relationship began to change the day Mason accidently walked into Khari's life. He was on campus as a guest speaker and wandered into the wrong class. Khari was asked to escort him to the right building and Mason was immediately mesmerized by her beauty. He begged her to stay for his speech and even though she wasn't taking that subject, convinced by his jaunty personality, she accepted. Khari was engulfed by Mason Holloway's confident demeanor. The way he grabbed the attention of a room full of people and owned it, not to mention he delivered a powerful speech. Khari found herself oddly attracted to him. Maybe it was the fact that he was older and seemed more knowledgeable then any man she had encountered. He spoke about things she had no idea of and it intrigued her. She agreed to exchange numbers with him and after a few weeks of phone tag she decided to meet him for lunch. One lunch turned into another, which led to dinner and eventually she was seeing him as much as possible.

Contacting Khari became hard for Sin. She would rarely return any of his calls or be on campus when he would show up to see her. She would tell him she was in study group or preparing for a play but the truth was she was spending her free time with Mason and enjoying every bit of it. The guilt never seemed to eat at her.

But after the newness and excitement of sneaking around began to wear off she slowly began to realize she didn't feel about Mason the way she did about Sin. But there was one thing Mason could offer that Sin couldn't: he was on the fast track to be governor someday and that was the safe cookie cutter life she always wanted. All the power without any of the danger, so she thought. Sin was merely a drug dealer and although he was good at it, how far would it get him, she thought to herself at night as she tried to provide answers for her conflicted heart. Did she want love and loyalty or power and stability; she would have to make a choice soon.

Sin had never spoken much about his father and siblings. Growing up he always knew who his father was but had no knowledge of what it was that he did. Sin always kept in contact with his sister Cassie, but he was never close to the Holloways. He always assumed his father really wanted no parts of him and his mother. But it wasn't until she died that he found out the truth. It was because of his mother's wishes that his father stayed away. She had always felt betrayed by him for keeping the fact that he was married a secret. Once she found out she wanted nothing to do with him. Marion respected her wishes but always tried to help her out monetarily but even that was a struggle, most times she would refuse his help altogether. She was strong and independent, providing for Sin through her job as a nurse at the local hospital. After she passed away Marion reached out to his son to try and establish a father son relationship. After initially being reluctant Sin gave Marion a chance, slowly building a bond. Marion took to his son fast, seeing a lot of himself in the young hustler. Word had begun to spread about Sin and his crew taking over Fort Green and the surrounding blocks. Marion felt his son had outgrown the corner hustle. It was time to open him up to the other side of his business dealings and convinced him to be a part of the family business and claim what was rightfully his.

Sin was adamant about keeping that part of his life away from Khari for the time being, deciding the less she knew the better. But he had every intention of one day explaining the power and position his father held in the state of New York, the depths of which he was just realizing himself.

Sin was slowly becoming aware that something wasn't right between him and Khari but even he couldn't have imagined the tangled web she had weaved. Everything eventually came to light one Sunday when Sin was invited to dinner at the large Holloway estate in Westchester. After being shown in by the butler, Sin was escorted through the double doors of his father's study, where

Marion was engaged in an intense conversation.

"They got exactly what they paid for, end of discussion." Marion yelled sternly into the phone before hanging up. Looking up seeing Sin he stated, "Business as usual."

Sin barely cracked a smile. "I thought the number one rule in business is the customer is always right," he sarcastically replied.

"No son, number one rule in this business is once the money's in your hands, never give it back," Marion said causing both men to laugh. "You're only a victim of the rules you live by, remember that."

Sin just nodded at the jewel he had just received from his father.

"C'mon," Marion said getting up out his chair. "I want you to come downstairs with me so you can meet your brother's new girlfriend. Pretty girl, smart too. Emma thinks she'll be a great look on his arm while he's running for city council.

Sin wasn't interested in meeting anyone Mason was dating. He really didn't care for him. Mason had made it clear from the beginning that he didn't accept the young man as his brother and wasn't thrilled about his recent involvement in the family business. He had known about his father's illegitimate child longer than any of the other siblings and due to the poisoning of Emma, he had decided he would never acknowledge him as family.

The two men descended down the stairs into the family room. Upon entering the room Sin was shocked to see Khari cuddled up on the couch with his brother Mason. This was why she had become *distant as of late. It all began playing back in his head like a movie, things all started to add up. He was enraged but managed to remain calm. It wasn't in his character to display his emotions for the world to see.*

Khari hadn't noticed the men enter the room. Mason had her full attention as he flirted and showered her with compliments. She had chosen the power and stability over love. She just needed to figure out a way to tell Sin. Something she planned on doing soon.

"Mason," his father called out getting his attention. "Introduce your girlfriend to your brother."

Mason stood to his feet with his chest out, proud to show off the new beauty in his life. "No problem Pops," he said every word dripping with confidence. "Yasin this is Khari, Khari this is Yasin…my father's son," reluctant to associate them as family.

The sound of his name being said blared in her ears like feedback from a speaker. Everything seemed to grind to a halt as she thought to herself, this can't be happening, but it was. This wasn't how she wanted him to find out but it was happening. How could she look up and look him in the eyes? She was too embarrassed, ashamed that she had been caught and with his brother of all people. She had tried to upgrade her chances at a successful life and now she stood on the verge of losing it all. She hoped it wasn't him but the sinking feeling in her stomach and the lump in her throat told her otherwise. Finally, she raised her head and stood up off the couch making eye contact with the all too familiar face.

"Hey how you doing?" Sin said sticking out his hand to greet her. "It's nice to meet you," he said.

"Khari is studying to be an actress," Marion bragged on her, tapping his son admiring her beauty.

"I can believe that," Sin replied with a backhanded compliment, sending her a subliminal message, letting Khari know he now saw her for who she really was— an opportunist.

Her mind seemed to be in overload. She couldn't muster up the strength to make her tongue move. Even if she could, what could she say? What kind of game was he playing pretending not to know her? That hurt more than being caught. Finally, she was able to force a smile and utter, "Nice to meet you too."

Sin didn't say a word to her the rest of the night while they ate dinner with the Holloways and he hadn't spoken a word to her in all the years since.

* * *

"Like I said, that's cool it's not important," Sin replied.

"Sin I know what it is that you do out there in those streets. You've always been official, since we were younger. I need you to do what you do and bring my daughter home to me. I know I have no right to ask you for anything but I beg you to bring her home to me. Please," Khari said before breaking down crying again.

Sin felt awkward, not really knowing what to do. He took a seat next to her and tried to offer her some form of assurance. "I'm gonna do whatever I can to make all of this right for Pops, Uncle Nate and Bria."

Khari missed the sound of his deep, melodic, baritone voice. She remembered how she used to find comfort in his words and could fall asleep to the sound of him speaking sweet nothings in her ear laying in the bed after sex. She remembered the butterflies he gave her when he would come around. She hadn't felt like that about her husband in a longtime and to think of it she had never felt like that about Mason. The tears began flowing faster as the choice she had made began haunting her. Looking at Sin sitting next to her reminded Khari of what could have been, really what should have been. But she was used to the guilt. It was something that she secretly dealt with every day for the past eight years.

"Sin I need you to promise me you will bring her back," she reiterated as she placed her hands on his face and moved closer to him.

"I will Khari. I will do what I can to bring her back," Sin said grabbing her hands and removing them.

"You have to Sin," Khari said leaning in attempting to kiss him. "She's your daughter," she confessed in a light whisper. The words left her mouth before she was able to stop them. Khari had sworn to take that secret with her to her grave but she had let it slip in a moment of emotional weakness.

Sin jumped to his feet with a look of shock on his face

looking at her with daggers in his eyes. "What the fuck are you talking about? What kind of game you playin' Khari?" he asked grabbing her by the shoulders picking her up off the couch.

"No game Sin, I've always known," she said as he let her go. "I was pregnant when I decided to be with your brother. It was the main reason why I chose him. I wanted my child to grow up with a father, not having to go visit him in jail or at the cemetery. That's where I thought you were headed...so I made my choice."

"And you didn't give me one," he said as all the hatred he once had for her quickly returning. "You got a lot of shit wit' you Khari. You did all that to protect her and look how it turned out," then he turned and walked out the door.

Khari fell back on the couch, placing her head in her hands and sobbing. She was too wrapped up in her emotions to notice Emma walk past the door. Eavesdropping in the shadows, she had only been a few feet away in the hallway and had overheard their entire conversation. Unbeknownst to Khari her most guarded secret had just fallen into the wrong hands.

Sin stalked down the hallway, his rage increasing with every step. In the middle of a war he couldn't afford his mind to be clouded with anything, not even the fact that he just found out he had a daughter. But no matter how much he tried to push it out of his mind Bria's beautiful face was all he could see. He thought about how he had missed out on seeing her born, helping her take her first steps or hearing her first words. He hated the fact that Mason had gotten to experience all of those things. Khari had stolen that away from him and that he could never forgive. He had watched Bria grow up from a distance, never knowing and it hurt. How could she do this? he thought while cursing Khari's name. Entering the kitchen, the look on his face spoke volumes even when his words didn't. Cassie was first to notice and spoke up.

"You ok?" she asked only to have to repeat herself after receiving no answer initially.

"Huh...Yeah...Yeah, I'm good," he said pretending nothing was wrong. He hadn't made up his mind as to what to do about what Khari had just told him so he decided to keep it to himself, at least for the moment.

"You don't look like you're ok," she said letting him know she wasn't buying his answer, but still deciding to switch subjects. "We're gonna stay here tonight, to be with Mase and Khari, and to help Mom out. What you gonna do? You want me to make up one of the guest rooms for you?"

"Nah," he said not wanting to be anywhere near his brother or his wife. "But I'll be close by," he assured her.

All the sashay in Ashleigh's walk was gone as she slowly strolled into the kitchen with the look of a prostitute after a long night of work. Her lips stick was faded and her mascara was smeared and running from all the tears of seeing her father all bandaged up in his bed. The thought of losing the man she looked at in almost a godly way had frightened her like nothing before and she was still visibly shaken.

"I need to get out of here," she whined. "It's too sad in here, I'll just cry all night if I stay. I'm going home."

"Everybody needs to stay close. We don't need nothing happening to anybody else in this family," Sin instructed.

"He's right," Elijah said rising from his seat at the breakfast bar joining the conversation.

"I'm not staying here. I don't care what you say Sin, and can't nobody make me. I'm grown," Ashleigh said

"I don't give a fuck what you do. I don't have time for ya shit right now," Sin snapped.

"I got it bruh. I'm heading back to the city now. I'll make sure she get home safe," Beans said as he entered the room overhearing their spat.

"See!" Ashleigh replied sneeringly.

"Whatever." Sin countered as he walked out the kitchen.

CHAPTER 24

"Yo, you real wild with the shit you be doin' ma," Beans said looking over to Ashleigh who sat in the passenger side of his Mercedes-Benz, ignoring him as she looked out the window and she rolled her eyes. "Seriously niggas go through a lot to make sure your spoiled ass is safe! Your father puts a lot of shit on that nigga Sin and all that shit trickles down to me cause I'm a nigga who is gonna make sure shit run smoothly for my man." Beans was noticeably upset and Ashleigh could tell by the flaring of his nostrils and the lines of frustration that formed on his forehead.

"What you don't understand Beans is that I don't need no tails or fucking security. I'm not a dumb bitch. I don't need my brother knowing my every move or my father or you for that matter!" Ashleigh snapped back with an attitude.

"Nah ma you are dumb!" Beans replied catching Ashleigh off her mark.

Her body language changed as she sat up in her seat and turned to face him prepared to give him a tongue lashing. "Who the fuck you think you talking to nigga? I'm—"

"You what?" Beans said cutting her off in mid snap. "You a little dumb rich girl who think money can buy her every muthafuckin thing. There's niggas out here getting killed every day 'cause they trying to tear down what we built. How far you think your name gonna take you shorty? That shit can open doors for you and that shit can take you to the grave."

Ashleigh sat quietly listening to Beans lecture her. In a funny way, his aggressiveness turned her on. She always thought that he was sexy with his caramel complexion and his thuggish ways and the scar on his face enhanced his sexiness to her. She knew that nigga wasn't scared of anything or anyone. He would bust his gun in broad daylight and wouldn't think twice, and the thought of that made her pussy wake up and throb a little. She never would consider the idea of fucking with him cause of her brother and up until recently she never would fuck with a hood nigga like him but since she started messing with Case she felt more carefree and knocked a couple of notches off her so called high horse.

"You poppin' up at my club with your home girls drawing attention to yaselves, got clown ass niggas all up in ya face."

"Psss," Ashleigh sucked her teeth and laughed. "What you jealous or something?" she looked at him seductively and bit down on her lip.

"Nah, ma I'm not jealous. I just watch shit. Trust me I don't ever have to be jealous of anyone. Anything I ever wanted...I got and if I didn't have it, there was solid reason behind it."

Beans pulled up to Ashleigh's high rise apartment building near Central Park and put it in park waiting for Ashleigh to get out of the car. After a few seconds he looked over at her to see why she hadn't gotten out. Ashleigh was staring out of the window with tears streaming down her face. Caught off guard, his first instinct was to reach out to her and console her but he just extended his hand to lift her chin up and to face him. All his anger quickly disappeared when he saw her crying. He didn't know if it was how he was talking to her or the string of recent events that was affecting her at that moment. But all he could feel was his heart palpitate at the sight of her tears. Beans always admired Ashleigh from a distance. He knew that with the line of work he was in, and the close friendship and partnership he had with her brother, it was seemingly impossible for him to try and be with her. So he always kept his feelings to himself. His feelings for her were a lot of the reason he kept a close eye on her, making sure she was always good and offering to do something when it involved her. It was almost like his way of being with her but not really being that. If the situation was different he would've definitely tried to make her wifey, taking her to a different level where she wouldn't be ruthless like her mother. He saw the potential in something that was so forbidden in his world.

"What's wrong ma? Damn I ain't trying to make you cry or nothing," Beans said to her in a more soothing tone then he had previously used.

"I'm just tired of all this shit. I feel like I got to live the life my father wants me to live instead of my own. Only be in certain places, associate only with certain people, because I'm Marion Holloway's daughter. Now look at him he's laid up in the house fucked up with bullets in him. How cautious can I be? How safe am I if they touched him?"

Seeing her frustration and pain, Beans pulled her into him using his free hand to wipe the running mascara streaming down her face. "I got you ma. I ain't gonna let nobody touch you. Ya hear me?"

The words that he said hit her heart fast. For some reason she knew he was serious and she felt he wasn't just saying that because it was his duty. She felt a side of Beans that she hadn't before; he genuinely had feelings for her and he was letting her see that side. Ashleigh, for the first time in a long time, felt safe and vulnerable. She looked up at Beans and kissed his bottom lip sucking on it before she pulled back. Beans started to stop her but couldn't help but welcome it as he pulled her closer and aggressively kissed her, introducing their tongues to one another. Ashleigh gripped his neck, trying to control the moment, but Beans wouldn't have it. He grabbed her and pulled her from her seat and she straddled his lap. The erection that formed in his True Religion jeans was at attention and Ashleigh grinded her pussy on it letting him know that she was aware of it and welcomed it. Beans hit the automatic button in his car to pull up the windows. His tinted windows left nothing for spectators to see and as Ashleigh took off her shirt and threw it in the back seat she went straight for his belt, loosening it, desperate to see his manhood in the flesh. His thick wood stood straight up at attention. He grabbed her breasts in one hand and grabbed a firm grip of her hair in another. He began to lick and suck softly on her neck, causing her nipples to harden and her pussy to get wet. Ashleigh pulled her skirt up over her hips and pushed her black Victoria's Secret panties to the side as she mounted Beans' dick and grinded vigorously on it until she felt the clicking sensation to her G-spot. Beans let his seat back and gripped a handful of her plump ass cheeks, making her grinding more intense by jerking her hips to the rhythm. Not a word was said, just the moans that came out of her mouth and the heavy breathing that came out of his. Ashleigh rode his dick until she creamed all over it and his thighs became slippery with her juices. Beans, turned on by her exploding on him, felt himself about to cum and lifted her up, shooting his load on her stomach.

Ashleigh leaned back on the steering wheel catching her breath and looking at the man who just took her to her climax. "You want to come up?"

The two of them exited the vehicle headed towards her building. Unknowingly to them, Case had tailed them since they left her parents' house. He wanted to see how everybody moved from a distance. He never drove off. He parked in a cut where only things were visible to him. When he seen, Ashleigh leave the house with Beans he followed them to see where they were headed. It heated him to see her get in the car with Beans. Beans, along with Sin, were on his radar and to see his bitch with him ate at him. The whole time Beans and Ashleigh was in the car Case was parked on the other side of the street seeing the whole show. It wasn't clear and a hundred percent visible to him but through the windshield he could see Ashleigh straddled on top of Beans.

"This fucking hoe ass bitch," Case fumed to himself as he reached in his dash for the box of Newports. He pulled on his cigarette steaming it like a blunt. He was vexed and what he saw only added fuel to his fire. "This bitch want to do a nigga like me dirty? I'ma fuck her whole world up." He flicked the square out the window and pulled his car out of park when he noticed the couple step out the vehicle and rode off undetected. He definitely was putting his plan into motion now with no remorse.

CHAPTER 25

Emma adjusted Mason's tie and brushed off the shoulders of his suit, making sure he was presentable for the cameras that awaited him on the other side of the door. The news' vans had been camped outside of his campaign headquarters for hours awaiting word on the incident involving his father and the kidnapping of his daughter. Though he and Khari were currently not on the best of terms, they both knew that it was important for them to show a united front. Bria's safe return was something that they both wanted as they prepared to make a plea to her captors on live television. Khari paced nervously as the time neared, trying to keep a firm grip on her emotions. The emptiness she felt in her soul was unexplainable and only Bria being returned to her could fill it. She watched as Emma tended to her husband. Her mother in law's obsession with Mason's image at the moment was turning her stomach. Lately the sight of either of them mad her sick.

"Make sure you look straight in the camera," Emma told him. "You want them to know you are still strong even in the face of tragedy. That whatever it is that they are trying to do to you and this family, it will not work and you won't be deterred from seeking election."

"What about my daughter? Your granddaughter. Do you even care about her?" Khari asked.

"What are you talking about now Khari, of course I do. I've been dealing with these types of things a lot longer than you, so it would serve you well to pay attention," Emma spat. "You need to speak from the heart. You will be the one who will be able to get to the kidnappers the most. A mother's love."

Khari just shook her head at Emma's need to be in control of everything. "Are you ready?" she said sucking her teeth and looking at Mason.

* * *

"Jimmmmmy!" the woman's voice echoed through the single family home in the upper middle class neighborhood in Queens. "Breakfast!" she screamed.

Jimmy Testa rolled out of bed and slid his feet into the pair of slippers waiting at his bedside. The once powerfully built enforcer for the Martello Family was now a rotund middle aged man. Although the years had added pounds to

Keys to the Kingdom

his waistline, they had also added clout to his standing within the family. He had moved up the ranks and was now the underboss of one of the strongest families in the country. He was seen as the quintessential gangster, tough, smart and silent, preferring to keep a low profile unlike his boss. But like Iron Mike Di Toro, he didn't shy away from using violence to get his point across. His reputation as the archangel of death was well known. Most importantly, Testa was an earner who brought in tons of cash for the family courtesy of his monopoly on the local unions. Through those unions he extorted payoffs, solicited bribes and enforced his control. He also was in possession of over two million dollars in contracts from the New York City Public Housing Authority. He oversaw most of the family's legitimate businesses, which he used to stash and clean most of their money. His understated demeanor was a perfect contrast to the more brash and cocky public persona of the family's leader. He understood and accepted his role, earning Di Toro's trust long ago. Testa played a key role for him during an internal struggle for power within the Martello family that he eventually won.

"Jimmmmmmy!" his wife screamed again.

"I'm coming," he finally answered her back, rising to his feet and grabbing his royal blue robe off the back of the closet door before slipping it on. Still half sleep, he slowly walked out into the hallway and down the stairs. The smell of bacon greeted his nostrils, further waking him as he entered the chef style kitchen. His wife, Celeste, stood over the stove putting the final touches on a large breakfast. She had become accustomed to cooking for her large family, which included three daughters and two sons, and continued to prepare huge meals even though they were all grown now and had long moved out. "Good morning hun," he said greeting her, followed by a kiss on the cheek.

"How'd you sleep?" she asked in her thick New York Italian accent. Celeste was the traditional mob wife, looking like the women on the VH-1 reality show, lots of hair and make-up. Jimmy always made sure she wanted for nothing. She had grown up in a neighborhood full of mobsters and enjoyed being part of the life.

"Like crap, my friggin' back is killing," he replied as he sat down at the kitchen table. "Where's the paper?" he asked looking around not seeing it.

"Oh shoot, I'm sorry I forgot to grab it," she admitted. "I'll get it now," she stated cutting off the stove.

"No, I got it."

"Eat your food before it gets cold," she insisted.

"It's alright," Testa said pushing back and standing up from the table.

Testa stepped out of his front door into what look to be the start of another gorgeous day. He descended the steps and marched down the long driveway towards the street. The neighborhood was quiet like it always was that time of morning; the only noise was the sound of birds chirping. The portly man finally reached the bottom of the driveway and was slightly out of breath. Spotting the paper laying in the street, he stepped off the curb bending over to retrieve it. He hadn't noticed Sheik stepping from behind a large tree gripping a gun with a silencer. A silent shot ripped through the back of the mobster's skull just behind his ear as he collapsed onto the street. Two more shots entered his body, making sure he was finished. Sheik unscrewed the silencer and calmly tucked the gun into his sweat suit jacket before jogging up the block into a waiting vehicle. Jimmy Testa lay dead in the street, a bloody mess and no one had seen or heard a thing.

* * *

Dominic and Frankie Gallo exited the diner in Bayside, Queens after enjoying a large breakfast and discussing some business, a daily routine for the brothers. The two made men were top ranked members of the Martello Family and looked the part. The Gallo's oversaw a crew of murderers, drug dealers and extortionist. Dominic, a playboy who bore a strong resemblance to JFK Jr., was notorious for his quick temper and would fly off the handle at moment's notice and commit murder. Although Frankie, the older and more physically built of the two, was mild mannered, he was just as deadly.

The brothers were known for kidnapping drug dealers and local businessmen then informing them that they had been paid to kill them. They would then demand a large payment not to follow through on the fake contract. Fearing for their lives and willing to do anything, most paid what they asked but those who foolishly didn't were brutally tortured or murdered. This level of ruthlessness made them star pupils in their boss' eyes and they quickly became his go to guys to carry out hits.

"Aye, don't forget we gotta pick up Vinnie on the way." Frankie reminded his younger brother.

"Fuckin' Vinnie, we're running late as it is." Dominic snapped. "Now we gotta pick that cocksucker up. You're killing me Frankie," he said angrily banging on the top of the car before getting in.

"Aye, I don't give a shit if you pick the fuckin guy up or not. It makes me no never mind," Frankie said opening the passenger door and getting in.

"You know we should whack that bastard anyhow," Dominic said out the blue.

"For what?" Frankie said laughing at his brother's statement.

"I don't fuckin' trust the guy...he sweats too much for me. His palms are always sweaty...I never trust a guy with sweaty palms. He's bound to rat on you," Dominic proclaimed.

"Fuck outta here!" Frankie screamed out in laughter at his brother's logic. "Whatta you talkin about."

"It's true," Dominic said laughing knowing how ridiculous he sounded. He started the car and backed out of the parking spot. Making a right out of the parking, he was immediately forced to stop at a red light.

"Sweaty fucking palms," Frankie said still enjoying a laugh, unable to believe what his brother said. "You know you're something else Dom. You wanna murder the poor guy over of his sweat glands."

The brothers shared a laugh while at the light, unaware of the two motorcycles approaching them on each side. As the motorcycles pulled alongside of the incognizant mobsters, they noticed the two young ladies with ample backsides straddling the back of each bike as the drivers crept to a stop. Dom eyeballed the ass of one of the women, letting his eyes stroll up her body until their eyes met through her helmet. He nodded his head, showing appreciation for her sexiness just as the two young ladies pulled out guns and opened fire. Bullets ripped through the car doors like a hot knife through butter, shattering glass and killing the Gallo brothers in the process, in broad daylight. When the hail of gunfire ceased, the motorcycles carrying Cairo and Egypt sped off around the corner and out of sight, leaving a gruesome massacre in their wake.

* * *

"We ask for the safe return of our daughter Bria. She needs to be home with us, amongst the people who love her and miss her so much," Mason said as his voice began to crack, betraying the strong exterior he was trying to present. "This is a trying time for my family and no matter the point you may be trying to get across," he continued looking directly in the camera while holding a picture of Bria for the world to see. "This beautiful little girl has nothing to do with it."

"Please bring her back to us," Khari cried out. "I miss her so much. She is so innocent and sweet. She doesn't deserve any of this, and we don't deserve this. Please bring my baby back..." she said before collapsing into Mason's arms as he held her, supporting all of her weight, pulling her away from the microphones and cameras back into the doors behind them as the detectives began taking questions from reporters.

* * *

Tommy "The Shark" Piccolo nervously paced back and forth constantly checking his watch every few seconds. It had been almost 48 hours since his wife had disappeared. He hadn't slept a wink since and he was rapidly coming apart at the seams at each passing moment. Tommy had always done everything in his power to make sure his "family life" didn't interfere with his family's life; keeping the two worlds completely separated. So he still couldn't wrap his mind around how they had located his family's home and snatched his wife on her way to the grocery store. Still and all, he was willing to cooperate if it meant her safe return. He followed all the instructions given to him by Sin, including being at the empty warehouse in the industrial park just over the bridge into New Jersey. The instructions said to be there at 10 o'clock and to come alone. Sin reminded him that any outside involvement of any kind would mean death for his wife, no exceptions. It was now twenty minutes past the hour and the nervous energy building in his stomach proved too much as he began violently vomiting his lunch from earlier in the day. Reaching inside his jacket he located a napkin and removed it, folding it once before wiping his mouth.

"Where the fuck are they?" he growled to himself. His mind filled with horrible images of what he knew could be happening to his wife. Being a loan shark and extortionist, he employed his own set of enforcers and knew the methods they used to get the things they wanted. As hard as he tried he couldn't seem to shake those thoughts out of his head. He looked towards the sky, saying a brief prayer hoping she would remain safe. His prayer concluded just as a set of headlights came speeding around the corner and screeched to a stop.

Sin and Beans hopped out the car approaching the grief stricken mobster.

"Dunna Dunna Dunna. What up Shark?" Beans joked walking up on Tommy. "Everything alright? You look a little sick playboy," he continued, noticing the man's pale face.

"Yeah I'm fuckin' great. Now where's my wife? I did

everything you'z guys said," Tommy barked upset not seeing her. "I gave you all the information I had on Di Toro and his people," he continued hoping at any moment she would appear. "I'm a man of my word."

"You sure about that?" Sin asked. "Di Toro's still breathing."

"I told you everything I know. I promise you," he pleaded with Sin.

"Calm down," Sin commanded. "You know what Tommy, I believe you," he said pulling his phone out and dialing. The phone rung once before it was picked up on the other end. "Put the wife on the phone," he said before handing it to the shaken man.

"Hello," he spoke into the phone, hoping to hear his wife's voice. The color began returning in his face as he heard the voice of the woman he had been married to for the last 10 years on the other end. He tried his best to reassure her that everything will be fine and repeated over and over how sorry he was and how much he loved her before handing the phone back to Sin, who hung up. "Now for that other little bit of business we spoke about," Tommy said now feeling a little better after hearing his wife's voice. "I'm gonna need to relocate after serving up the underboss of the family to you'z guys," he whispered, looking around nervously, as if someone could hear him speak the words of betrayal.

Sin nodded in agreement, opened the backdoor of his car,

reached inside and pulled out a large black duffle bag. Beans shook his head as Tommy started to rub his hands together anticipating the large pay off he was about to receive. The greed was evident on his face. He could hear the sounds of the water splashing against the shore on the beautiful beaches in the Dominican Republic playing in his ear. The five hundred thousand dollar payment would seem 10 times that in DR and he would have his choice of women to choose from when it's time to find a new gumar.

Sin put the bag on the hood of the car. "There's something else I need to know."

"Anything," Tommy said just wanting to get his hands on the cash and be on his way.

"The little girl, where is she? Where they keeping her?" he asked, the seriousness in his tone matching the look on his face.

"I don't know. I swear," Tommy said feeling nervous that his answer might not be good enough, but he was being truthful and hoped Sin could recognize it.

"Ok," Sin said disappointed and slightly angered with the lack of information. "I'll let you do the honors," nodding towards the bag on the car and stepping aside.

"Don't mind if I do," Tommy said unzipping the bag. His eyes lit up at the sight of all the Benjamin Franklin faces staring back at him. He began pulling them out by the stack, happy to hold them in his hands. He had never been in possession of so much money at one time. He fingered through it, smelled it than fingered through it again. "I must say Sin, you are truly a man of your word," Tommy said banging two stacks of money together in his hands.

"You know it's a funny thing about money," Sin said.

"What's that?" Tommy asked never taking his eyes off the overstuffed duffle bag.

"It only buys a man's silence for a short time."

"Huh," a confused Tommy said looking up from the money trance he was in.

BANG!

The back of Tommy's head suddenly exploded like a watermelon smashing into the ground, leaving his brains splattered everywhere. As his body collapsed to the ground, Beans stood over him holding his gun and squeezed two more shots into his lifeless body for good measure.

"But a bullet buy it forever," Sin calmly finished his statement before turning to his friend. "Damn Beans, you couldn't do it a lil' cleaner," he barked looking down at the blood splattered on his shirt. "Come on let's dig a hole," he said popping the trunk removing a pair of shovels, tossing one to Beans before removing his shirt and tossing it in the trunk. "I ain't trying to be out here all night." Sin hit call back on his phone and waited for it to be answered once again.

Ali picked up quickly seeing Sin's number. "What's good?"

"No loose ends," he replied.

"No doubt, I got you," Ali said before hanging up the phone. He walked over to his brother Barkim, who stood with his gun trained on Tommy's wife as she sat tied to a chair sobbing and blindfolded.

"What's up?" Barkim asked.

"No loose ends."

"What?" Barkim questioned. "That wasn't part of the plan."

"Plans change."

"Nah, I'm not doing it son," a defiant Barkim spat tucking his gun into his waist and attempting to untie the woman. "That's against the rules."

"Nigga they touched homie's family, this is war...ain't no rules!" Ali reminded him.

"Nah, I ain't with this. I'm not doing it," he said as he headed for the door.

"You buggin nigga," Ali yelled to his brother as he disappeared through the door. Ali pulled out his gun and squeezed a single shot into the woman's head knocking her over in the chair. He stepped closer and fired once more.

CHAPTER 26

Marion was recovering and would soon be able to resume command of the Holloway organization. Sin and his regime had successfully staved off defeat at the hands of Iron Mike Di Toro and the Martello family at least for the time being. Although he couldn't claim victory as of yet, Sin had struck a major blow in the war between the two factions and their counterblows had weakened as of late. With Marion on the mend, it would only be a matter of time before the tide swung their way completely. By protecting his father's empire, he had proven what Marion had known all along; that he was the most suitable heir to the Holloway Empire. Their enemy had come to the same conclusion and knew that the only way to avoid complete defeat was to kill Sin before Marion could fully heal. Sin was naturally a tactical genius, something Di Toro had underestimated, and with the help of his father he was slowly becoming a brilliant strategist. Marion at full strength with Sin by his side as his second in command, their enemies wouldn't stand a chance. Sin alone had succeeded in sending Di Toro into hiding, but it came with a price. He was now a mark with a contract on his head. He was extremely cautious with all his movements and had purposely avoided attempting to make contact with Ariane in order to preserve her safety. It pained his heart having to keep his distance but it was necessary. He had already lost enough in the bloody war; having to bury a number of his henchmen and couldn't afford for anything to happen to her. Bria was still missing and nobody knew if she was even alive, it had been weeks since they had heard anything. Mason had paid a ransom to a group of men claiming to have her only for the police to discover it was all a fraud. The men were trying to scam money out of him and his wife, playing on their vulnerability. Sin silently dealt with her disappearance. He had yet to spill the secret of her being his daughter, not even to Beans, but it was slowly burning him up on the inside.

Beans was holding his own secret after sleeping with Ashleigh, and was trying to decide if telling Sin was the right thing. After all she was grown and capable of making her own decisions. It was a subject that had never been discussed between the two friends but Beans had always seen it as an unspoken rule, one that he had now broke. He knew he had to eventually come clean; keeping a secret from his nigga wasn't in his blood. In the business they were in, withholding the smallest secret could be seen as a sign of disloyalty, something he didn't want to occur. He had strong feelings for Ashleigh, but not enough to allow it to cause a rift between him and Sin. The two sat in silence in the living room of the penthouse in the fancy hotel on Park Avenue, waiting for everyone to join them. It was the night of the election and even though he could truly care less about Mason's run for mayor, keeping the family safe was his priority.

Ten floors below was a room full of supporters anxiously awaiting the results of tonight's election. Holloway for Mayor signs were everywhere throughout the room, along with swarms of balloons and men and women sporting pins with the same phrase on them; all waiting for Mason to emerge victorious and turn the watch party into a celebration.

For his part Mason hadn't shown his face in hours. He had yet to move from the spot in the master bedroom with his eyes glued to the TV, watching the votes as they came in. Marion too had a front row seat next to his daughter-in-law, as a nervous Emma paced back and forth in the room. Every family member was scattered throughout the elaborate space dealing with the uncertainty in their own way. Elijah exited the kitchen with a bottle of Ciroc in his hand and Jewlz not too far behind holding glasses.

"I don't know about y'all but all this suspense is killing me. I need a drink," he said sitting the bottle down and grabbing one of the glasses from Jewlz. "Y'all drinking with me?"

"Hell yeah," Beans said snatching a glass from Jewlz.

"I know you ain't drinking lil bro?" Sin asked shooting the young man a look.

"Nah, not my thing," Jewlz said.

"He ain't old enough to drink anyway," Elijah joked.

"How old is you lil nigga?" Beans asked.

"22," he replied proudly.

"Nigga when I was 22 I was drinking, smoking, fucking," Beans proclaimed. "You is fucking right?" he said causing the men to laugh.

"Yeah," Jewlz chuckled. "I'm fucking."

"How's it going at business school?" Sin asked. "Pops pulled a lot of strings to get you in there. You not fucking up are you?"

"Hell no, Pops would kill me," he assured. "Plus Cassie stay on my ass about how important it is that I learn all the ins and outs of the casino business."

"Y'all niggas serious about this casino shit," Beans said.

"Yes I am," a voice said. The men looked up to see Marion gingerly making his way towards them. "At least that's the plan."

"You good Pops?" Sin said rising to his feet racing over to help him.

"Yeah I'm fine," he said refusing his help and giving him a look before taking the empty seat left by him jumping up.

"With the help of Mason and my son in law," he said pointing to Elijah. "Along with my other political influences, I plan on eventually building a casino right here in New York City. I just need the laws changed so I can move forward with the project. That's why Mason winning this election is so important. I've already secured Jewlz a position at Foxwoods working with a high ranking executive where he'll be able to learn the business first hand. My plan is to finance the project with family's money only, nephew." Marion concluded letting Beans know that he acknowledged him as part of the family.

For the first time Sin could see that Beans was taking the opportunity as a serious one. Hearing Marion's plan had him thinking the impossible could be possible. "What kind of investment you talking Unc?"

"We can discuss all that when the time is right. Now is somebody gonna pour me a drink?" Marion asked cracking a smile.

"Dad they're about to announce the results," Cassie screamed sticking her head into the room.

"Jewlz hurry up, turn on the TV." Marion instructed.

* * *

"Mason! Mason! Mason!" The scene in the ballroom was a triumphant one as a victorious Mason stood on stage soaking up the cheers from the crowd. He had just achieved the biggest accomplishment of his career and was trying to take it

all in, but the emptiness he felt made it bittersweet. Bria's absence had dulled the moment. The thought that he may have only won due to the sympathy vote from her being kidnapping was a hard pill to swallow. Still he stood there with a forced smile, preparing to make a speech; his very first as mayor of the great city of New York. He took a deep breath and stepped to the microphone as the crowd gradually lowered the volume on their chant in order to hear the man of the hour.

"Thank you to all of you for being here with me tonight. I will never forget this moment and I promise I will never let you down. I ask that you keep me and my family in your prayers. And I thank you for deciding that this city needed a change. This is only the beginning of great things to come," he said raising his hands in victory as the cheers began again. "Mason! Mason! Mason!"

Khari stood on stage off to the side watching as her husband basked in his glory. She was truly proud of him, but after everything they had been through to get to this point she really didn't know how to feel. Her daughter was missing and she was unhappily married to a man who was merely a puppet: for his father's financial gain, his mother's greed and now for the city of New York. Everybody had their hands on one of his strings except her. And she knew it was only going to get worse from here. The smile on Emma's face as she stared at Mason let her know, if she hadn't already.

Emma clapped as he walked off the stage straight to her with a grin on his face. He was now mayor but still needed her approval, a confirmation that he had done well. And she was more than happy to oblige. "You did great son. I'm so proud of you," she said followed by a kiss on the cheek leaving traces of her lipstick on his face. "You are what a Holloway man is all about," she fed his ego. "A leader of men. You did it. And I love you."

"I love you too Ma," he replied returning her kiss with one of his own on her cheek. "Where's Pops?"

"He's seated over there," she pointed. "You know he's still recovering and he needed to rest."

Mason made his way over to his father who was beaming with pride watching him walk towards him. Mason loved that look. It was something he hoped to see a lot more of now that he had done what they had set out for him to do. Being able to stand strong, weather the storm, and still come out victorious he knew he had finally gained some of his dad's trust but more importantly his respect. Maybe now he would see fit to involve him more in the full operation of the Holloway Empire. The powerful position he now held was surely to be viewed as an asset to his father's reign.

"We did it Pops," he boasted as he took a seat next to the elder Holloway.

"You did son," he replied. "You made this happen. Be proud of yourself because I'm so proud of you. I've always been proud of you Mase."

"Nah, Pops we did this," Mason repeated.

"I might have laid the plan out but you executed it and that was the hard part. You did all the heavy lifting."

Mason nodded his head, elated to hear the words his father was speaking to him. He had always felt the pressure of living up to being the eldest son of the great Marion Holloway and for the most part he felt he had fallen short. But to hear his father was proud of him meant everything to him. "How you feeling? You ok?' Mason inquired.

"Yeah I'm good. I wouldn't have missed this for the world," he smiled.

Sin and Beans blended in with the crowd while keeping a close eye on the family. They had henchmen all over the room just in case anything went down. It was still war time and they had to take extraordinary precautions with tonight's event. They refused to get caught slipping this time. Sin stared in the faces of every person in the room trying to detect if someone from the Martello family had infiltrated the celebration. He knew Di Toro had been too quiet as of late and would be looking for a chance to regain some ground in the war. Scanning the room, his eyes locked on one of the servers, something about him wasn't right and set off alarms in Sin's head. He got Beans attention and pointed the young man out. The two quickly moved in on him, inching closer and closer as he made his way through the crowd directly towards where Marion and Mason were sitting. Weaving through the crowd as fast as possible trying to gain ground, they noticed a second server heading in the same direction. Beans headed for one as Sin took the other. The first server began to reaching into his waist and Sin simultaneously did the same while quickening his pace. As the young man removed his hand from his waist Sin caught the glimpse of the white towel he had removed just as he bent down to retrieve a broken glass off the floor. Sin stopped himself from pulling out his weapon at the last minute and watched the young man take the piece of the broken champagne flute into the back. Sin spun his head around quickly trying to locate the other server, but didn't see him nor Beans. His head was on a swivel darting his eyes back and forth trying to see where they had disappeared to. Beans emerged from the kitchen and shook his head letting his partner know it was nothing. Sin took a deep breath, relaxing a little just as he heard Cassie's voice on the microphone.

"Hey everybody can I have your attention," she spoke loudly. "My family would like to thank you all for showing my brother so much love and support throughout this entire campaign, and we would like to make a toast to not only my brother, but to you, the campaign workers and supporters."

To Sin's dismay all the servers started coming around the room with champagne filled flutes as people began to take one. Making it impossible for him to keep his eyes on all of them. He made a beeline over to where his father and brother were sitting now joined by Emma and Ashleigh, just as Mason was helping Marion to his feet. The waiter came by and handed each one of them a glass. Sin declined when it was him turn, more concerned with studying faces.

"Here's to you Mason and a successful run as mayor of this city!" Cassie shouted with her glass raised in the air, getting a cheer from the crowd before taking a sip as everyone followed suit.

"So Yasin, where's your pretty little friend? I'm surprised not to see her here. I really liked her." Emma mocked knowing that she had been the cause of he and Ariane's spat.

Sin just shook his head ignoring her attempt to engage in conversation. He was done playing her game and felt he deserved more respect than she was giving after backing the Martello family down, preserving her lifestyle in the process. The days of being polite out of respect for his father were quickly coming to an end for her. Mason refrained from joining in on his mother's attempt to agitate like he usually had. The encounter at the hospital was still fresh on his mind. Sin looked him in his face, and seeing he wanted no problems, he offered a congratulation then nodded his head.

"Thank you," Mason replied.

Marion smiled. It was the first time in forever he could remember the two of them being cordial with one another. Emma offered a fake smile as well.

"I'll be right back," Sin said. "I'ma bout to go check Beans for a second."

The group continued their discussion, sharing a laugh or two. Quite suddenly, Marion felt as if the room began to spin. The air seemed to thicken, making it hard for him to catch his breath. Saliva filled his mouth faster than normal as he started having difficulty swallowing. Marion's body grew weak and his grip on his champagne flute loosened.

Sin walked up on Beans almost undetected. "Nigga stop staring and say something to her," he said.

"What?" Beans had briefly lost himself in his thoughts and hadn't realized he had been staring at Ashleigh from across the room.

"Nigga you think I don't know you got a thing for Ash," he said. "That shit obvious and I know she have a thing for you since way back. If you like her like that, say something to her."

"You good wit' that my nigga?" Beans asked still unsure of what his friend's true feelings were.

"Y'all grown my nigga, that's on y'all. I know what type of nigga you is, you A1. So it is what it is. You feel me?" Sin said as he gave a pound to his man just as the sound of a glass hitting the ground and a blood-curdling scream rang out.

The entire room turned to see Emma standing over Marion's body, tears running down her face, as Mason kneeled next to him trying to somehow assist him. Marion's body shook violently as foam oozed from his mouth. Sin raced over to him followed by the rest of the Holloway children as supporters backed back giving them room. Kneeling next to him, Sin reached out and grabbed his hand. Marion attempted to squeeze it but his body was failing him and he had no control over his muscles. His body continued to shake uncontrollably as his family stood by helplessly in shock. Marion stared into Sin's eyes. The look on his face told his son he wanted to speak but couldn't. Both men were professional death dealers and could feel the reaper lurking. The look was all too familiar to Sin. He had seen it on the faces of men who took their final breath at his hands. Finally, his father's body stopped moving as a smirk appeared on his face and his eyes rolled back in his head and closed. Marion Holloway was dead. He had been poisoned. Sin rose to his feet immediately and scanned the entire room for the server that had handed Marion the glass of champagne, but he was nowhere to be found; in all the celebration he had slipped out undetected. All the Holloway women kneeled next to the body, crying until the coroner arrived and placed a white sheet over the patriarch of their family before lifting him onto a stretcher and carted him out of the hotel. Mike Di Toro had succeeded in taking the most important piece off the chess board.

CHAPTER 27

The view through the floor to ceiling windows of the Manhattan skyline on a sunny New York City day still wasn't enough to put a smile on Sin's face. As he sat on the edge of his king size bed in the luxurious one bedroom condo in Williamsburg, that overlooked the East River, staring at the custom tailored suit laid out on the bed next to him. It's funny how the mind works, whereas a certain smell or taste or just the sight of something can bring you back to a place from your past, good or bad. For Sin, it was the sight of the black suit on the bed. Although he owned more than his share of the fine Italian garments, he was not a big fan of them. They reminded him of all the losses he had suffered throughout his life. Having to put one on always took him back to the very first time he could remember having to wear one. His attention immediately shifted to the picture that sat atop his nightstand, causing him to reach out and grab it. The picture, taken in the mid 90's, was of a young Sin and his mother; a gorgeous brown skinned woman who looked to be in her early thirties. The low haircut she sported at that time was an instant reminder to him of the chemotherapy treatments she had endured trying to fight off the cancer she eventually succumbed to at the age of 36. Years had passed since his mother's funeral, but his disdain for suits hadn't. Those memories didn't seem so distant today as he found himself in the familiar position preparing for another funeral. Normally stoic and able to bury his emotion deep within, he was having a tough time keeping them under wraps at the moment. Though his eyes would not drop a single tear, the pain he felt was obvious with just a look into them. He was mentally and physically drained. The events of the past few months had worn on him more than he cared to acknowledge. Brief moments like this, alone in his bedroom, were the only times he was afforded the chance to assess the magnitude of his situation. After all he wouldn't dare show an ounce of weakness out in the streets. The beast that was New York City would swallow him whole. Looking out the window once again at the tall buildings that lined the sky across the water and trying to find something that would start his engine, he was reminded of something he had been told only weeks before. *"Content is a crown seldom kings enjoy."* And with that thought, he rose to his feet and began getting himself dressed, fully prepared for whatever the day would bring. Hidden underneath the fine Italian fabrics of his suit was a grizzled veteran of the streets. A calculated thinker unafraid to do whatever it took to be victorious.

* * *

Sin pulled off the main road onto a less traveled side street, parking his car and cutting off the engine. The remote location outside the gates of the cemetery gave him a clear view, not only to the graveyard but the main road as well. He was able to see who was coming and going. He had been parked for 15 minutes when three black SUV's turning into the cemetery caught his attention making him sit up in the driver's seat to get a better look. Through the slightly tinted windows of his black Jaguar XJ, he watched as the hit on Iron Mike Di Toro played out. Like a conductor of a symphony, Sin had just orchestrated a masterful piece of work. In wiping out the Martello family, his team of killers had proven they could get to anybody.

Satisfied with the outcome he checked his rearview, adjusting his tie and placing his glasses on his face. Sin had somewhere he needed to be and he was already running late, something he hated. Jay-Z's "Say Hello" began playing as he started the car and merged into flowing traffic as police cars with the sirens blaring raced the opposite way towards the deadly scene at the cemetery. Iron Mike's death had ended the tug of war between the two factions and signaled a changing of the guard. Yasin Kennedy was now the leader of the strongest organization in the city.

CHAPTER 28

The death of Marion Holloway sent shockwaves through the underworld, not only in New York, but around the country. He was looked at as somewhat of a mythical figure in the streets; a black gangster who dealt with the Italian mob not as a peon but from a position of power. Not since the days of Bumpy Johnson had there been a black mobster held in such high regards. Marion was the man everybody came to for help, and never were they turned away or disappointed. Never did he make empty promises, or use the excuse that his hands were tied by more powerful people than him. He had a way of making things happen for people. All of these people and many others had come from all over to see him laid to rest.

* * *

Just down the block, parked on the opposite side of the street, Case sat in the driver's seat of his car with a gun in his lap and a clear view of the front of the church. Unimpressed by the goings on and undeterred, he sought only vengeance. He knew he was at an extreme disadvantage, but Ashleigh was his ace in the hole. She could get him close enough to Sin that he could put a bullet right between his eyes. The Holloways had just suffered a great loss but in his mind their mourning had only just begun. Case tucked his weapon before stepping out the car and adjusting his suit making sure it was concealed properly. He was prepared to enter the lion's den and would do so without hesitation.

He entered the packed church and found a seat near the back, positioning himself closest to the aisle; a perfect spot with a view of the front and easy access to the exit. Case sat back waiting for the funeral to start with a devilish grin on his face; he was about to get his payback.

* * *

Sin pulled up just in time to join the rest of the family as they prepared to enter the church. Mason linked arms with Emma, escorting her up the steps and through the double doors of the church with Khari and MJ at his side. Cassie and Elijah followed close behind with her boys each holding one of her hands. Jewlz had his arm around Ashleigh, her head was buried in his shoulder with tears streaming down her face as he slowly guided her up the steps. Sin sported his normal emotionless facial expression as he walked behind his younger siblings, occasionally rubbing Ashleigh's back trying to soothe her but she was inconsolable. Their leader was gone and for the first time the Holloway children's perfect world was in disarray. Their hearts were heavy and the emptiness they felt had robbed the joy from their lives. Marion had meant so much and to so many, but none more than them. Although Sin had exacted revenge in the name of their father, it did nothing to ease the pain they all felt.

Sin had now lost both his parents and thoughts of his mother's funeral replayed in his head as he made the trek up the steps. Her death was far less extravagant but just as painful for him. He could still remember it like it was yesterday. That also was the last time he had stepped foot inside a church and he readied himself as he prepared to do it all again. Reaching the top of the steps, he heard a voice from behind call his name and turned to see who it was. To his surprise Ariane stood at the bottom of the steps in a black stretch jersey draped dress and matching pumps. Sin walked back down the steps meeting her halfway, her mere presence allowing the smallest bit of sun to shine in on his darkened mood, bringing a smile to his face.

"Whatchu you doing here?" he asked surprised and relieved at the same time.

"This is where I belong," she spoke softly. "By your side," she said using her hand to stroke the side of his face.

He grabbed her hand and placed it to his lips, kissing it gently. Her answer was what he needed to hear at that moment. He pulled her to him and kissed her passionately. For Ariane, time seemed to stand still. No one or nothing in the world mattered for that brief moment as they stood on the church steps with their lips locked together.

"C'mon," Sin said grabbing her hand and leading her up the steps into the church.

The funeral was royal and the church was packed. All the top street bosses from around the country came to pay their respects, along with executives, politicians, celebrities and every member of Marion's organization. Phil Catanzano was in attendance, he had come to say goodbye to his old friend, as did what was left of the other Five Families. The war had decimated the once mighty coalition. Most families had splintered into small crews and were engaged in power struggles for the kingdoms left behind by their fallen leaders.

* * *

Case watched as Mason and Emma entered the church first. He had never laid eyes on the matriarch of the family but immediately knew who she was. She was elegant and he could see that her beauty had once rivaled Ashleigh's in her younger days. It was now apparent where she had acquired her looks. Cassie and her family followed and once again he could see the resemblance. The Holloway women were all gorgeous but there was no doubt that Ashleigh stood head and shoulders above the group. As she entered the church all eyes were on her, even in a disconsolate state she was exquisite. Their eyes met and he offered a faux smile followed by a nod. She tried returning the gesture but couldn't seem to make her lips cooperate. She lowered her head burying it back into Jewlz's shoulder, not wanting to see her father lying in the casket at the end of the aisle. As she turned away Case clinched his jaw tight and hatred flowed through his veins. It had been their first encounter since he had seen her and Beans in front of her building. It bothered him more than he cared to admit, but seeing Ashleigh with another man had only added to his appetite for retribution. He could feel his adrenaline pumping as his eyes landed on the man he wanted nothing more than to kill. Case held himself partly responsible for the death of his friend; it had haunted him every day since. He knew nothing could bring Dre back, but spilling the blood of those responsible would make him feel a little better. Sin hadn't actually pulled the trigger. Kyrie had but that meant nothing to a man blind with anger. He was owed a debt and eventually they would all pay but today was Sin's day.

Unaware of the close threat, Sin passed right by Case on his way down the aisle. The war had been costly to everyone involved. They had all suffered great losses and there were truly no winners. But as Sin approached the beautiful white and gold casket and looked down at the man he was a spitting image of, he felt like the biggest loser. No one had paid a bigger price than him and his siblings. They hadn't just lost a

Don of a family like the rest. They had lost their father. Ariane had never seen the look in Sin's eyes before as he stared down at his fallen leader. She knew he was hurting and squeezed his hand, wishing she could take away his pain. She would place it on her own heart if it meant he wouldn't suffer. Finally, Sin stepped to the side taking his seat along the front pew next to the rest of the family with Ariane beside him, just as the pastor began to speak.

* * *

The white horse drawn hearse led a small group of cars into the cemetery. Marion was to be buried in a much smaller, more private ceremony than at the church. Only family, members of his organization, and those he had done direct business with were allowed to attend. Emma stood silent in front, surrounded by her children, tears slowly rolling down her face. Her pride and stubbornness wouldn't allow her to show the world the full amount of grief she felt inside. But reality had finally set in as she watched the casket of the man she spent the last 37 years of her life loving being lowered into the dirt. Emma was strong but a lot of her strength had come from the confidence of knowing she was the wife of a powerful man. Emma always held Marion down with every decision and every move he made. She took pride in her name and her family. There was nothing she would not do to make sure their legacy remained. The thoughts of their years together replayed in her mind. Emma was a queen, but the days she spent as a nickel and dime hustler's wife were vivid; all the risks she took, all the secrets she kept, even the betrayal she had accepted but most importantly the undeniable love they shared. There was nothing Marion Holloway would not do to make her happy and there were no limits Emma wouldn't go to ensure his. She reveled in her position and found comfort in the safety Marion's status provided something she had always viewed as impregnable. That invincibility had now been shattered. Emma had seen his rise and reaped every benefit of his reign, now she was trying to handle the burden of his fall with the same gracefulness.

Mason's admiration for his mother only grew watching her endure their loss with great fortitude. She had always been the backbone of the family and he now found solace in her strength. As he prepared for the biggest challenge in his life, the first he would face without Marion there to guide him so having Emma by his side was of grave importance. He was where his father had always dreamed he would be— mayor of the city. He smiled knowing that Marion was able to witness it before he passed.

Ashleigh was a different story. She struggled to find the silver lining in it all. There was only sorrow, pain and heartache for her. She had invited Case to join her family at the cemetery and had her head buried in his chest since they arrived. Case pretended to care, rubbing his hand over her hair trying to provide comfort. Every eye was locked on the regal casket being lowered into the ground but his were focused only on Sin, who stood away from the rest of the family surrounded by members of his crew with Ariane at his side. Case gritted his teeth as he patiently waited for his chance to take him out.

Sin stood watching his father being returned to the earth. Since the church, his face had not changed but he now allowed a single tear to escape his eyes and roll down his cheek before wiping it with the back of his thumb. Sin never realized just how much love he had for Marion. He had always seen him as a mentor more than a father. Marion hadn't played a big part in his life growing up but had managed to make a huge impact on him as he transitioned to manhood. Sin was thankful for the lessons and knowledge he had equipped him with over the years and even more appreciative for the time they had been able to spend together. He was broken from his thoughts by his shoulder being brushed up against by Mason as he positioned himself next to him. Neither man showed the other the respect of making eye contact, just remained looking straight at the mourners as they tossed single white roses on top of the casket in the ground before exiting.

"You know now that Pops is gone your services are no longer needed. I'll be taking over from here," Mason coldly stated as he continued staring forward. "So after this, you and your little crew can disappear. You're no longer welcome in my mother's house." Mason leaned in to add emphasis to his next statement. "Oh and if...you were mentioned in the will, I'll make sure someone contacts you. But no worries right? We all know you're not hurting for anything," he chuckled amusing himself. "By the way, all the political connections and police protection you were afforded under Pops just went in the ground with him. Now that I'm mayor, I advise you cross all your T's and dot your I's, correctly. Cause the first chance I get to put you under the jail, I gladly will."

Sin's blood boiled at the sound of his brother's voice. He knew Mason was never built to handle any of his father's affairs and would have a tough enough time running the city without Marion to guide his every move. The bitch in him was blatant, and although he wanted to break him down right there, he decided not to out of respect for the funeral. Sin let out a slight chuckle then leaned in towards Mason to make sure he could be heard clearly.

"You always been a smart dumb nigga, you know that right?" he rhetorically asked. "Look to your right playboy," he instructed. Mason and Sin both turned towards the group of men who stood at attention, waiting for Sin's signal to move. Amongst that group were Sin's young niggas and Marion's old henchmen. "Now look to your left." There stood Catanzano and the rest of the families paying their respects to Emma. Phil looked up and nodded to Sin who returned the gesture showing an unspoken respect. "This my kingdom ma'fucka,"

Sin squeezed his brother's shoulder and walked away leaving Mason to stand alone with his anger.

EPILOGUE

Sheik's heart pounded in his chest as he weaved his truck in and out of traffic, speeding through red lights in route to the hospital.

"Slow down," Maleekah screamed in between rhythmic breaths as she dealt with the contractions from being in labor.

Sheik ignored her request dipping the truck from lane to lane once again before turning into the hospital and slamming on the brakes in front of the emergency room. Jumping from the truck he quickly raced inside to get help and returned with an orderly. He opened the passenger door assisting her out of the vehicle and into the waiting wheelchair. Sheik grabbed the baby's bag from the backseat and followed them into the hospital. He was about to be a dad again.

* * *

Sin felt a tap on his shoulder and turned to see Phil Catanzano. He nodded his head signaling for the mob boss to step away from the group so the two of them could talk. Once the men were out of earshot of everyone else, Catanzano began the conversation.

"Me and your father go back a longtime," he said staring off into space, shaking his head as he reminisced. "He was a good man and we made a lot of money together, maybe too much money. It's like the richer he got, the more relaxed he became. Years ago, a bum like Di Toro could have never gotten to him."

"My father was a great man, but he was still just a man, and he did as all men do...the best he could. So picking apart his mistakes is not something I care to do. My only concern is the future of this family. And since I'm not my father, we don't have the history you two did. So movin' forward I'd like to know where you and I stand?" Sin questioned.

"Well, I offer you the same thing I offered your father many years ago, my friendship. Our lives and our fortunes depend greatly on our friendship," he explained. "Denying a favor asked by a friend, no matter how small, could be seen as a sign of hostility. Favors are not asked lightly therefore they can't be refused lightly either. You understand?"

"Perfectly," Sin said extending his hand to shake Phil's.

"And as a sign of my friendship," Phil said as the two shook hands. "I got some information I think you'll be interested in. Someone in your circle is not as trustworthy as you would like them to be.

Sin looked suspiciously at Catanzano, questioning the validity of his statement. "You sure about that?"

"Positive," he nodded. "I don't have a name yet but I know for sure there's a rat inside your organization," he proclaimed then turned signaling his men and heading for his vehicle.

Sin rubbed his hand over his face and exhaled a deep breath, then turned his attention to his crew. He wanted to believe that none of his niggas would ever snake him. After all, they had come up together and were now stronger than ever. But he knew better, the game had shown him too much. He had seen the tightest crews fall apart. Power, money and jealousy were a deadly mixture and had contributed to most niggas downfall. Sin would respect if one of his niggas was to come for his head but he could never respect a coward who folded under the alphabet boy's pressure and bit the cheese.

* * *

Emma was still accepting condolences when Sin and Catanzano's meeting caught her eye. She had quietly taken notice of everyone's treatment of Sin, acting as if he was the new head of her fallen husband's empire. *How dare them,* she thought. *The dirt on my husband's grave is still fresh and his bastard is getting fitted for his crown.* Her blood boiled at the sight of the two men speaking. Having seen enough, she motioned for one of the bodyguards to escort her as she made her way to the waiting limousine.

* * *

Finally, Ashleigh had managed to gain control of her emotions, but her eyes were swollen and red from all the crying she had done. Cassie hugged her little sister then whispered in her ear. "You know you're still beautiful right." She knew that it would make her smile and it did as she pulled back seeing Ashleigh's pearly whites for the first time in days. "Now that's my girl," Cassie said delighted to cheer her up. "Ash, this is Ariane, Sin's girlfriend."

"Hi," Ariane said with a smile. "Nice to meet you."

"Likewise," Ashleigh said returning a smile.

"Who's this?" Cassie asked referring to her sister's handsome guest.

"This is my friend Case," she replied.

"Hello," he said greeting everyone while trying to keep an eye on Sin who was talking to a burly Italian man. "Sorry for your loss," he offered his empty condolences. As he stood engaged in conversation with the group, they all noticed Emma storming past in route to the limousine. "I see your moms is taking it pretty hard huh? How long were your parents together?" he asked pretending to be interested as he bided his time, waiting for his opportunity to present itself.

* * *

"What was all that about wit Catanzano?" Beans asked as Sin

approached.

"Nothing, he just wanted to know where we stand," Sin said not wanting to indulge the information he had just received. He was still processing it and needed time to formulate a plan to bring the rat out into the light. "Yo where's Sheik?" he asked noticing his absence and using it to change the subject.

"I don't know. I haven't heard from him all day," Kyrie said.

"Me either," Beans said.

Sin looked at Barkim and Ali but they just shook their heads as if to say them either. Sin knew something was wrong. It wasn't like Sheik to disappear like that. His mind immediately replayed what Big Phil had just told him. "Anybody tried calling him?" he asked calmly, anxious to know his whereabouts but not wanting to arise any suspicion as to what he was thinking.

"I'm on it right now," Ali said with his phone to his ear.

Ariane smiled as she made eye contact with Sin while making her way over to him, she was still happy that she had decided to show up. And from the look on Sin's face he was too. He looked at her like no man had ever before. It was like he could look straight into her heart and soul and see all the love she had for him. The look sent chills through her body and tingles between her legs. Her strong feelings for him scared her and intrigued her at the same time. She couldn't understand why she was so drawn to him. All she knew was that she wanted more; more love, more sex and more time spent with his strong arms wrapped around her.

"Everything aight?" he asked as she finally made it over to him.

"Yeah, everything is fine," she assured him.

"I'm just gonna be a few more minutes then we can leave," he informed her.

"Ok."

Beans eyes were trained on Ashleigh, but more so on the nigga standing next to her. He had vaguely remembered seeing his face before but couldn't pinpoint it. But that really was the least of his concern. After him and Ashleigh's encounter he had hoped to make something more out of it, but seeing Ashleigh with the next nigga had him vexed. It was obvious she didn't want the same thing. Beans found a small bit of humor in the irony, she had chased him for so long and now the energy had shifted.

"Beans," Sin said breaking his concentration. "I need everybody to meet at your club in a few hours. 6 o'clock," he said looking down at his watch.

"Aight," Beans nodded never losing sight of Ashleigh.

* * *

Sheik exited the hospital with a giant smile plastered across his face. He was the proud father of a brand new baby boy.

Every man's dream was to have a son he could instill life lessons in, give him the game and mold him into a great man. Sheik now had his and he beamed with pride as he strutted towards his truck with his chest poked out. Sheik slid into the front seat and began searching for his phone. After locating it, he saw a ton of missed calls and already knew who they were from. He dialed and waited for the phone to be picked up on the other end.

"Yo," he said hearing Sin pick up on the other end.

"Yo, where the fuck you at nigga?" Sin barked.

"I'm at the hospital. Maleekah went into labor on our way to the funeral this morning."

"Oh shit, for real?" Sin asked as his tone changed now excited for his friend's new addition. "What she have?"

"A boy nigga, I gotta lil' man now!" Sheik shouted into the phone overjoyed by the birth of his son.

"Congrats playboy. Whatchu name him?"

"Najee."

"That's what up. We all meeting up at the Bean's spot tonight around 6. We gonna celebrate, bottles on me."

"No doubt."

* * *

Emma shimmied over in the backseat of the limo and instructed for the bodyguard to close the door and wait outside. She removed her phone from her clutch, dialing a number and placing it to her ear.

"Hello," a voice said on the other end as the phone picked up.

"How much longer do I have to put up with this disrespect?" Emma spewed her venom into the phone. "My husband's bastard is being hailed as some sort of heir to his throne. He's no heir; he's not even a Holloway. I want him dead! Do you hear me? Dead! And all of his little ghetto minions too. Why isn't this done already?!"

"I'm handling it but it's not as easy or as simple as you may think. These things take time," the voice said.

"Time," Emma hissed. "Psss, maybe I've just got the wrong man for the job."

"You shouldn't underestimate me, Emma."

"And you shouldn't me. My husband made the same mistake and it was his last. There's nothing I won't do to get what I want or to protect this family's name. Now I served you Marion on a platter and you missed. So I took it into my own hands and got it done. Now if you wanna keep our deal intact, you'll have to start living up to your end of the bargain. Now I want Sin and his crew dead," Emma commanded like the evil queen she was.

"Not a problem. One more question," the voice said. "What about your granddaughter?"

Emma paused before answering. Thinking back to the conversation she had overheard between Sin and Khari, the gears in her twisted mind begin churning. "Hold on to her for a little bit longer. I may have another use for her after all."

Emma hung up the phone just as the limo door swung open and Khari got in followed by Mason. Emma pretended to wipe away tears, drawing more sympathy from the couple.

"You ok Mrs. Emma?" Khari asked sympathizing with her mother in law's loss. She understood sort of what the woman was dealing with after feeling her own pain and emptiness from Bria being missing.

"Yeah, you alright ma?" Mason asked.

"Yeah I'm fine. I just miss your father so much," she said letting her words trail off and her voice crack while summoning a few tears to sell it. "I'm just ready to go home."

"Say no more, driver to the house," Mason barked out.

* * *

Sheik pulled out of the parking lot into traffic. He hadn't made it a block when he saw the flashing lights from the unmarked car behind him. He switched lanes and turned down a relatively quiet block before pulling over. That gave him just enough time to put his gun in the stash spot. He rolled down his window and waited for the officers to approach. In his rearview he could see the two detectives exiting their vehicle and making their way towards his truck. One on the passenger side and the other creeping up on his driver side. When the detective on his side was close enough that Sheik knew he could hear him, he began trying to talk himself out of the situation.

"I'm sorry detectives if I was speeding. My wife just gave birth to a baby boy and I'm a little excited," he said in his most harmless voice but received no answer.

Sheik looked in the side mirror at the detective approaching his window and noticed the man had stopped moving.

"Our boss sends his condolences," the detective said catching Sheik's attention.

"Oh shit," Sheik yelled as he tried retrieving his weapon from the stash but it was already too late. The two men opened fire. The sound of bullets ripping through the doors could be heard as the men emptied their guns into the car, more bullets hitting Sheik than missing. When they were done the man on the driver's side opened the door allowing Sheik's bloody body to fall out onto the street.

* * *

"We gonna celebrate, bottles on me," Sin said before hanging up, then turned to his crew with a smile on his face.

"What up, what's going on?" Beans asked, anticipating an answer.

"That was Sheik, he at the hospital. Maleekah had the baby. A little boy named Najee." Sin bragged as if it was him.

The crew erupted with joy. They were all happy for Sheik

and couldn't wait to meet up with him later. There was gonna be a lot of cigar smoke and liquor sipping going down in the city tonight.

Ariane tapped Sin on the shoulder. "I'm gonna get ready to go. You go out and celebrate with your boys. I'll be waiting for you tonight," she smiled seductively.

"Nah, I'm coming with you right now," he replied before turning back towards his crew. "I'll meet up with y'all later," he said. "Let me go say goodbye to my sisters and I'll meet you at the car," Sin said kissing Ariane on the cheek. He followed behind her admiring her shapely figure. He missed making love to her and was ready to get out of there and reacquaint himself with her body. But first he made a pit stop joining the group that included Cassie, Elijah, Ashleigh and her guest that she had yet to introduce to him. Ariane continued on to her vehicle, waving goodbye to the group as she passed.

"I'm outta here," Sin announced interrupting the group, then kissing Cassie on the cheek. "I'ma see you this week. I gotta drop something off to you," he informed her then gave a pound to her husband. Sin looked at Ashleigh and opened his arms. She jumped into them, giving him the tightest hug ever. "Everything gonna be alright lil' sis," he reassured her as she squeezed tighter.

"We just been going through so much. I don't wanna lose you either," she said refusing to let him go.

"I ain't going nowhere," he laughed. "You can believe that."

"Oooh," she said suddenly remembering she hadn't introduced her guest to him. "Sin this is my friend Case. Case this is my brother I told you about, Sin,"

"What's good," Sin said offering a head nod.

"What up," Case said barely returning the gesture.

Sin could feel the frigidness in his response but decided to pay it no mind. He knew Case could tell the difference between him and the rest of his siblings and maybe felt the need for the tough disposition. Sin chuckled on the inside knowing that with just one wave of his hand, the cemetery they currently stood in would become Case's permanent residence. Ashleigh switched niggas like shoes so he didn't expect him to be around much longer anyway.

Jewlz walked up on them just as Sin was stepping away. "Hey lil' bro, walk with me," he said, followed by a head nod.

Sin walked towards the white Range Rover he had given to Ariane months before, talking with his youngest sibling. Jewlz idolized him so he hung on his every word. Sin knew it and took their moment alone to reaffirm some of the things he knew Marion would want for Jewlz.

"Even though Pops gone, nothing with you changes. You still gon' finish school and you still taking that position at the casino. He was depending on you and now I'm depending on you," he stopped walking and turned to face him. "Me and

Cassie. You ain't gonna let us down right?"

Jewlz shook his head. "Nah."

"I ain't think so," Sin said as he gave him a pound and a hug. "I got faith in you boy," he encouraged as he threw a couple of light jabs to his chest. "I love you." Sin concluded as he walked off.

"I'm about to slide myself," Case said. "It was nice meeting y'all, under the circumstances and all. I'm gonna call you later," he said before kissing Ashleigh on the cheek. Case stepped away from the Holloways and quickened his pace, trying to make up ground between him and Sin. Sin did him a favor when he stopped walking in the middle of his talk with Jewlz, allowing him to close the distance on his unsuspecting victim. Case slid his hand to his waist where he had tucked his gun back at the church. He had kept his poker face on all day, playing his cards just right and now he had the drop on Sin. Brushing up against Jewlz as he passed, he took a few more steps before reaching for the gun in his waist.

Sin advanced towards the Range Rover in his signature stride, unaware of the fast approaching danger at his back. He had just started crossing the path to where Ariane was parked when he heard the gravel from the road crunching beneath someone's feet stalking towards him. His senses told him something wasn't right, the swift thuds of the footsteps felt threatening. He reached for his gun, turning on a dime, making eye contact with his pursuer.

Case was caught off guard. He froze with a puzzled look on his face now staring down the barrel of Sin's gun and threw his hands up in a defensive manner, "Yooo, I—" Case begin.

Just as Ariane's Range Rover exploded sending both men flying through the air...

About the Author

Raised in Peekskill, NY, Ty Marshall is an undeniable talent with a highly skilled pen. Discovered by New York Times Selling Authors Ashley & JaQuavis, his ability to seamlessly weave authentic depictions of the street with great storytelling sets him apart from the pack. He is widely considered one of the rising African American authors in the country. Ty has independently released several titles which include: Keys to the Kingdom, 80's Baby and Eat, Prey & No Love. He also released a ebook through St. Martins Griffin entitled Luxury & Larceny. Ty is a proud husband and father that currently resides in Atlanta, Ga.

www.TYMARSHALLBOOKS.com